The Essential Catfish Cookbook

The Essential Catfish

 PINEAPPLE PRESS, INC.
Sarasota, Florida

Cookbook

Janet Cope and
Shannon Harper

Inquiries should be addressed to:

Pineapple Press, Inc.
P.O. Box 3899
Sarasota, Florida 34230
www.pineapplepress.com.

LIBRARY OF CONGRESS CATALOGING IN PUBLICATION DATA
Cope, Janet
     Essential catfish cookbook / Janet Cope and Shannon Harper.—1st ed.
         p.   cm.
     Includes index.
     ISBN 1-56164-201-0 (pbk. : alk. paper)
     1. Cookery (Catfish) I. Harper, Shannon, 1937– II. Title.

TX748.C36 C67 2000
641.6'92—dc21   00-034692

First Edition
10 9 8 7 6 5 4 3 2 1

Design by Carol Tornatore Creative Design

Table of Contents

Introduction: Celebrating Catfish   11

Acknowledgments   13

1. Down Home Cookin'
Fabulous Fried Catfish the Easy Way

Hints for Frying Perfect Catfish   16

Traditional Southern-Fried Catfish   18

New South Fried Catfish   19

Oven-Fried Catfish   20

Beer-Batter Catfish Fingers   21

Sesame-Fried Catfish   23

Tempura-Fried Catfish   24

Spicy Buttermilk-Fried Catfish   26

Fried Catfish Nuggets   27

Not Your Daddy's (Fried) Catfish—
Hints for Healthy Eating   28

2. Uptown Eating
Catfish Dishes with an International Flair

Catfish Piccata   32

Breezy Caribbean Catfish   33

Teriyaki Catfish   35

Tangy Lime-Peppercorn Catfish   36

Athenian Broiled Catfish   37

Tequila-Lime Catfish   38

Catfish Provençal   39

Mexicali Catfish   40

Riviera Catfish   41

3. Up-a-Lazy-River Recipes
Microwaving, Grilling, and Poaching Catfish the Easy Way

Hints for Microwaving, Grilling, and Poaching Catfish   44

Polynesian Catfish   45

Ginger-Garlic Catfish   46

Rosemary Catfish   47

Incredibly Easy Breaded Catfish   48

Catfish Isabella   49

Oriental Grilled Catfish   50

Lemon-Basil Grilled Catfish   51

Easy Italian Grilled Catfish   52

Easy Poached Catfish   53

The Literary and Lyrical Catfish—
Memorialized in Story and Song   54

4. Jambalaya and Fun on the Bayou
Cajun and Creole Cuisine

Cajun and Creole Cooking   58

Catfish Gumbo   59

*Keeping Catfish Fresh and Sassy—Hints for Buying
and Storing Catfish*   60

Catfish with Remoulade Sauce   61

Catfish Jambalaya   62

Creole Catfish   63

Blackened Catfish   64

5. A Baker's Half Dozen
Six Easy-Bake Recipes

Hints for Baking Catfish   66

Herbed Parmesan Catfish   67

Campfire Catfish   68

Crispy Catfish   69

Sunny Catfish   70

*Catfish Tidbits—Everything You Ever Wanted to Know
about Farm-Raised Catfish*   71

Catfish Baked in Mushroom-Wine Sauce   72

Summer's Garden Catfish   73

6. Soups and Such

Five Soups and a Sandwich

Hints for Making Fish Stock   76

Carolina Catfish Soup   78

Catfish Corn Chowder   80

Mediterranean Catfish Stew   81

Oriental Noodle Soup   83

Expandable Catfish Stew   84

Spicy Catfish Sandwich   85

7. Catfish Condiments

Remoulade and Other Saucy Accents

Hints for Storing Herbs and Spices   88

Easy Remoulade Sauce   90

Quick Tartar Sauce   91

Cilantro Tartar Sauce   92

Spicy Red Sauce   93

Low-Fat Horseradish Sauce   93

Basic Barbecue Sauce   94

Honey-Mustard Dip   95

Hooked on Catfish—Anglers Lure the Elusive Prey   96

Tzatsiki Sauce   97

Low-Fat Yogurt-Mint Sauce   98

Low-Fat Yogurt-Dill Sauce   98

Summer Salsa   99

Fried Catfish Dip   100

8. Catfish Companions

Coleslaw and Hoppin' John, to Name a Few

Pond Draining—A Time for Feasting   102

Quick Coleslaw   103
Moravian Coleslaw   104
Lynda's Easy Potato Salad   105
Old-Fashioned Potato Salad   106
Tangy Potato Salad   107
Anything-Goes Marinated Salad   108
Black-Eyed Pea Salad   110
Hoppin' John   111
Sweet Southern Dills   112

9. Foreign Friends

Great Side Dishes from Around the World

Availability of Ingredients   114
South-of-the-Border Salad   115
Greek Salad   116
LaDonna's Cheese Strata   117
Tuscan Bread Salad   118
Tabouli   119
Oriental Cucumber Salad   120
Oriental Coleslaw   121
Italian Tomato Salad   122

10. Amazing Maize

Cornbread, Hushpuppies, and Grits

All about Cornmeal and Grits   124

Anne's Alabama Cornbread   126

Mary Lynn's Never-Fail Cornbread   127

Hushpuppies   128

Tennessee Hushpuppies   129

Tennessee Baked Cheese Grits   131

Easy Stovetop Cheese Grits   132

11. Sweet Inspirations

A Fitting Climax to Down-Home Cookin' and Uptown Eating

Triple Chocolate Cake   134

Saint Paddy's Day Pie   135

Lemon Icebox Pie   136

Aunt Lila's Pecan Pie   137

Equivalents and Substitutions

Helpful Hints on What's What   139

Index   141

Introduction: Celebrating Catfish

In the South, catfish has long been a favorite food with a light, mild, sweet, and definitely nonfishy flavor, but catfish is no longer merely a regional dish. Since 1988 in the United States, catfish popularity has risen 50 percent, skyrocketing sales to one-half billion dollars a year. Nutritious and delicious catfish has come into its own.

There are catfish festivals, catfish restaurants, catfish aquarium exhibits, a catfish institute, a National Catfish Month (August), a U. S. submarine named Catfish, a catfish magazine for the more than ten million catfish anglers, and even a catfish line dance. Southern authors have memorialized catfish, and contemporary American chefs have revealed the fish's palate-pleasing properties.

The Essential Catfish Cookbook is designed to be user friendly, with recipes rated Very Easy, Easy, and Moderately Easy. Ratings are based on both the complexity of the recipes and the amount time spent in preparation. Recommendations from contributors and test cooks were taken into consideration. All recipes are within the skill level of beginning cooks.

Ingredients are fresh and simple and are likely to be on hand in most kitchens. Also, this collection of recipes encompasses all occasions—a grilled-catfish supper by the campfire, a casual Sunday lunch, an elegant dinner party. Notes sections are included so you can record your own changes to the recipes. This may be particularly helpful if you experiment with different kinds of cooking oils or spices and herbs. For example, if you decide to substitute basil for oregano (because that's what you have on hand), make a note of the results. So enjoy the recipes and make them your own;

substitutions and additions are definitely encouraged. As you use the book, we hope you'll be amused and amazed by the informative tidbits—little-known facts, lore, and legend—about the fascinating catfish.

One of the best parts of writing a cookbook is doing the research. Cookbook research takes you beyond the realm of libraries and the Internet and into markets and restaurants. We've sampled everything from delectable fried catfish with curry sauce in a Thai restaurant to smoked catfish sushi. We encourage you to do a little exploring in your favorite restaurants. You'll be amazed at what you'll find, and we hope that you will be encouraged to bring your ideas home and experiment.

Bon Appetit!

Janet Cope and Shannon Harper

Acknowledgments

First, our thanks to David and June Cussen of Pineapple Press for supporting this project. Thanks also to all those friends who critiqued and contributed, complimented and cooked for us: Donna Ball, Ann Barton, Mary Lynn Bell, Sophia Clikas, Kathryn Coumanis, Jim Crowley, Dana Davis and family, Paul Duke, Alice Enright, Val Spence McIntyre, Anne McMahan, Latanja McNay, Donna Pass, Margaret Pierson, Mary Jane Rivers, Linda Scott, L.L. and Valrie Spence, Lynda Tatum, Jerry and Cindy White.

A special thank you to Stacie Harris and Elizabeth Hedrick, to Phillip Lott for his initial research into the catfish culture, to Ann Wooten for her recipes and her time in the kitchen, to Carol Tornatore for her artwork and design, and to our editor, Kris Rowland.

This is truly a group project, and we could not have done it without you.

1
Down-Home Cookin'

Fabulous Fried Catfish the Easy Way

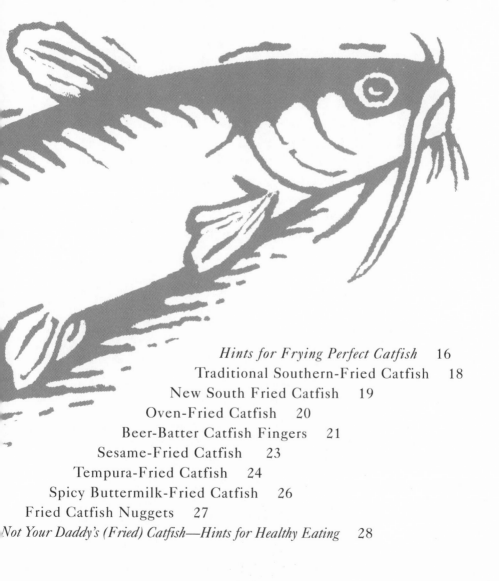

Hints for Frying Perfect Catfish 16
Traditional Southern-Fried Catfish 18
New South Fried Catfish 19
Oven-Fried Catfish 20
Beer-Batter Catfish Fingers 21
Sesame-Fried Catfish 23
Tempura-Fried Catfish 24
Spicy Buttermilk-Fried Catfish 26
Fried Catfish Nuggets 27
Not Your Daddy's (Fried) Catfish—Hints for Healthy Eating 28

Hints for Frying

1. Use a cooking oil with a high smoke point, such as peanut oil. Experiment with different oils to find the one you like best. Corn oil and peanut oil have a slightly nutty taste. Canola and soybean oils may have a hint of a beanlike flavor. Olive oil and sesame oil are usually too intensely flavored for frying fish but may be used in small amounts to enhance flavor.

2. For best quality, as well as safety, do not reuse cooking oils. Oils that have been heated to a high temperature and contain food particles turn rancid faster. The high temperature also lowers the smoke point, which increases the risk of the fat's bursting into flame. If this happens, smother the fire by putting a lid over the pan. Baking soda or salt will also extinguish a small flame. Never pour water on a grease fire.

3. Use a heavy skillet, preferably a cast-iron one. Fish cooked in a thin, metal skillet is easily burned. A heavy skillet distributes heat more evenly. A cast-iron Dutch oven also works well for frying catfish.

4. Choose a pan large enough for the fish to be cooked in one layer without crowding.

5. Add enough oil to the pan to ensure the catfish has a little buoyancy in the oil. Fish that sits on the bottom of the pan is more likely to burn. Fill a heavy skillet half full of vegetable oil or shortening. Add oil to a depth of at least 1½ inches when using a Dutch oven.

Perfect Catfish

6. Use kitchen tongs for dipping, dredging, and frying catfish (unless you enjoy the hands-on approach).

7. Cook catfish at 375° or over medium-high heat. A deep-fat thermometer will give the less-experienced cook more consistent results. Experienced cooks say they can tell whether the oil is hot enough by sprinkling a few drops of water in the oil and listening to the water sizzle and sputter. Be forewarned that the water turns to steam and may cause hot oil to pop out of the pan.

8. Immediately after cooking, drain catfish on paper towels placed over a layer of newspaper or a brown paper bag. If you are cooking several batches of catfish, put drained catfish on a wire rack placed over a baking sheet. Keep hot in a 200° oven until all fish is cooked.

9. Commercially prepared batter and coating mixes for fried fish are available at most supermarkets. Occasionally, seafood restaurants package and sell their special mixes, so experiment and enjoy.

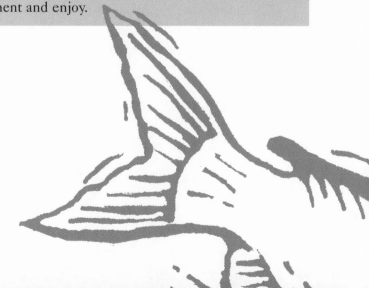

Traditional Southern-Fried Catfish

This is the catfish served at fish fries and fish camps all over the South.

Very Easy
Serves as many as you want

Yellow or white cornmeal
Salt and pepper to taste
Catfish fillets or whole catfish (gutted)
Vegetable oil or shortening
Lemon wedges or sauce (optional)

1. Combine dry ingredients in a shallow bowl or pie pan.
2. Rinse catfish under cool, running water and pat dry with paper towels. (Cut 3 slits in each side of whole fish before cooking.)
3. Dredge catfish in dry ingredients. Shake off excess.
4. Fill a heavy skillet half full of vegetable oil or shortening. (When using a Dutch oven, add oil to a depth of at least 1½ inches.) Heat oil to 375° (medium-high heat).
5. Fry catfish in a single layer 2 to 4 minutes on each side, turning once, until fish is golden brown and flakes easily when tested with a fork. (Cooking time will vary depending upon the thickness of the fish).
6. Drain fish on paper towels placed over a layer of newspaper or a brown paper bag.
7. Serve with lemon wedges or sauce, if desired (see Chapter 7, Catfish Condiments).

New South Fried Catfish

The addition of cayenne and garlic gives this fish a special flavor.

Very Easy
Serves 4 to 6

¾ cup yellow or white cornmeal
¼ cup flour
1 teaspoon salt
1 to 2 teaspoons cayenne pepper
½ to 1 teaspoon garlic powder
4 to 6 catfish fillets, 4 to 6 ounces each
Juice of lemon or lime
Vegetable oil or shortening
Lemon or lime wedges or sauce (optional)

1. Combine dry ingredients in a shallow bowl or pie pan, adding cayenne pepper and garlic powder depending on your taste for spiciness.
2. Rinse catfish under cool, running water and pat dry with paper towels. Drizzle fresh lemon or lime juice over fillets.
3. Dredge fillets in meal/flour mix. Shake off excess.
4. Fill a heavy skillet half full of vegetable oil or shortening. (When using a Dutch oven, add oil to a depth of at least 1½ inches.) Heat oil to 375° (medium-high heat).
5. Fry catfish in a single layer 2 to 4 minutes on each side, turning once, until fish is golden brown and flakes easily when tested with a fork. (Cooking time will vary depending upon the thickness of the fish.)
6. Drain on paper towels placed over a layer of newspaper or a brown paper bag.
7. Serve with lemon or lime wedges or sauce, if desired (see Chapter 7, Catfish Condiments).

Oven-Fried Catfish

This recipe gives the taste of fried fish without frying.

Very Easy
Serves 4

¾ cup cornflakes, finely crushed
1 tablespoon sesame seeds
¼ teaspoon onion powder
¼ teaspoon paprika
¼ teaspoon pepper
4 catfish fillets, 4 to 6 ounces each
Vegetable oil or cooking spray
Lemon wedges or sauce (optional)

1. Heat oven to 400°.
2. Combine cornflakes, sesame seeds, and seasonings in a shallow bowl or pie pan.
3. Rinse catfish under cool, running water and pat dry with paper towels.
4. Brush a light coat of vegetable oil on fillets or coat with cooking spray.
5. Roll fillets in cornflake mixture.
6. Place catfish on a foil-lined baking sheet lightly coated with vegetable oil or cooking spray.
7. Bake 10 to 20 minutes or until fish is no longer translucent at its thickest part and flakes easily when tested with a fork. (Cooking time will vary depending upon the thickness of the fish.)
8. Serve with lemon wedges or sauce, if desired (see Chapter 7, Catfish Condiments).

Beer-Batter Catfish Fingers

Beer and catfish always go together.

Moderately Easy
Serves 4 to 6

2 cups all-purpose flour, divided
1 teaspoon garlic powder
1 teaspoon cayenne pepper
½ teaspoon salt
½ teaspoon black pepper
8 ounces beer
Dash of hot pepper sauce (optional)
4 large catfish fillets, cut into strips
Vegetable oil or shortening
Dipping sauce (optional)

1. Add 1 cup of flour, garlic powder, cayenne pepper, salt, and pepper to a shallow bowl. Mix well.
2. Place second cup of flour in another shallow bowl. Gradually whisk in beer. Blend into a smooth batter. If you like a spicier fish, add hot pepper sauce to the batter and stir well.
3. Rinse catfish under cool, running water and pat dry with paper towels. Cut fillets into finger-size strips, 1 to 2 inches wide.
4. Dredge catfish fingers in dry ingredients and then in beer batter.

Catfish are prolific.

Worldwide, there are about twenty-two hundred species of catfish. North America is home to only twenty-six species, while South America boasts over twelve hundred.

5. Fill a heavy skillet half full of vegetable oil or shortening. (When using a Dutch oven, add oil to a depth of at least 1½ inches.) Heat oil to 375° (medium-high heat).
6. Fry catfish strips a few at a time 2 to 4 minutes on each side, turning once, until fish is golden brown and flakes easily when tested with a fork. (Cooking time will vary depending upon the thickness of the fish.)
7. Drain on paper towels placed on layers of newspaper or a brown paper bag.
8. Serve with a variety of dipping sauces, if desired (see Chapter 7, Catfish Condiments).

Catfish are diverse.

Of greatest commercial importance in the United States are catfish of the genus Ictalurus, meaning "fish cat." The channel catfish (spotted catfish) is I. punctatus, and the blue catfish (chucklehead) is I. furcatus. Commercial channel catfish are harvested at about 1½ pounds, but their cousins, the big blues, can weigh from 90 to 120 pounds. According to sports fishermen, blues can weigh as much as 150 pounds.

Catfish get their name from barbels (feelers) around their mouths. The whiskers are covered with taste buds to help the fish find food. In fact, catfish have taste buds all over their bodies, even their tails.

Catfish are sensitive.

Sesame-Fried Catfish

The secret of this recipe is the addition of sesame oil to the egg bath.

Easy
Serves 4

¾ cup all-purpose flour
1 teaspoon cayenne pepper
4 to 6 tablespoons sesame seeds
2 eggs
1 teaspoon sesame oil
4 catfish fillets, 4 to 6 ounces each
Salt and pepper to taste
Vegetable oil or shortening
Hot pepper sauce (optional)

1. Mix flour, cayenne pepper, and sesame seeds in a shallow bowl. In another bowl, beat eggs and whisk in sesame oil.
2. Rinse catfish under cool, running water and pat dry with paper towels. Salt and pepper fillets.
3. Dip fish first in egg bath, then dredge in flour/sesame mix.
4. Fill a heavy skillet half full of vegetable oil or shortening. (When using a Dutch oven, add oil to a depth of at least 1½ inches.) Heat oil to a temperature of 375° (medium-high heat).
5. Fry catfish in a single layer 2 to 4 minutes on each side, turning once, until fish is golden brown and flakes easily when tested with a fork. (Cooking time will vary depending upon the thickness of the fish.)
6. Drain on paper towels placed on a layer of newspaper or a brown paper bag.
7. Serve with hot pepper sauce, if desired.

Tempura-Fried Catfish

Try this as a hot appetizer or as a main course. Be sure to use cold water as specified.

Moderately Easy
Serves 4

½ cup plus one tablespoon flour
1 tablespoon cornstarch
½ cup ice-cold water
1 egg yolk
3 large catfish fillets, cut into strips
Juice of 1 lime
Salt and pepper to taste
Vegetable oil or shortening

Sauce:
¼ cup soy or teriyaki sauce
1 teaspoon fresh ginger root, minced
2 cloves garlic, minced, or ½ teaspoon garlic powder

1. Blend flour, cornstarch, water, and egg yolk together in a shallow bowl. Batter will be lumpy and the consistency of thin pancake batter.
2. Rinse catfish under cool, running water and pat dry with paper towels. Drizzle each fillet with fresh lime juice; sprinkle with salt and pepper. Cut fillets into finger-size strips, 1 to 2 inches wide.

North American catfish belong to the family amiuridae, peculiar to the continent. Fossils in Wyoming date from the Eocene period, forty to fifty-four million years ago.

Catfish are old as the hills.

3. Dip strips into batter a few at a time.
4. Fill a heavy skillet half full of vegetable oil or shortening. (When using a Dutch oven, add oil to a depth of at least 1½ inches.) Heat oil to 375° (medium-high heat).
5. Fry catfish strips a few at a time 2 to 4 minutes on each side, turning once, until fish is golden brown and flakes easily when tested with a fork. (Cooking time will vary depending upon the thickness of the fish.)
6. Drain on paper towels placed on a layer of newspaper or a brown paper bag.
7. Mix together soy or teriyaki sauce, ginger, and garlic or garlic powder. Serve with catfish.

Spicy Buttermilk-Fried Catfish

The secret of frying is to have the oil at the right temperature so the crust will be golden brown. This recipe is good as an entree or served on a sandwich bun with remoulade sauce.

Very Easy
Serves 6

¾ cup buttermilk
½ cup white cornmeal
½ cup all-purpose flour
1 to 1½ teaspoons cayenne pepper
6 catfish fillets, 4 to 6 ounces each
Salt to taste
Vegetable oil or shortening
Lemon wedges or sauce (optional)

1. Pour buttermilk into a shallow bowl.
2. Mix cornmeal, flour, and cayenne pepper in a separate bowl.
3. Rinse catfish under cool, running water and pat dry with paper towels. Sprinkle with salt.
4. Dip catfish in buttermilk, then dredge in flour mix.
5. Fill a heavy skillet half full of vegetable oil or shortening. (When using a Dutch oven, add oil to a depth of at least 1½ inches.) Heat oil to 375° degrees (medium-high heat).
6. Fry catfish in a single layer 2 to 4 minutes on each side, turning once, until fish is golden brown and flakes easily when tested with a fork. (Cooking time will vary depending upon the thickness of the fish.)
7. Drain fish on paper towels placed over a layer of newspaper or a brown paper bag.
8. Serve with lemon wedges or sauce, if desired (see Chapter 7, Catfish Condiments).

Fried Catfish Nuggets

This is a treat for adults and kids alike.

Easy
Serves 4 to 6

½ cup yellow cornmeal
1 teaspoon salt
½ teaspoon pepper
1 teaspoon chili powder
½ cup buttermilk
1 egg
4 large catfish fillets, cut into 1½-inch nuggets
Vegetable oil or shortening
Lemon wedges or sauce (optional)

1. Mix dry ingredients in a shallow bowl or pie pan.
2. In a separate bowl, whisk together buttermilk and egg.
3. Rinse catfish under cool, running water and pat dry with paper towels. Cut into 1½-inch nuggets.
4. Dip catfish nuggets into milk/egg mixture, then into cornmeal mixture.
5. Fill a heavy skillet half full of vegetable oil or shortening. (When using a Dutch oven, add oil to a depth of at least 1½ inches.) Heat oil to 375° (medium-high heat).
6. Fry nuggets a few at a time 2 to 4 minutes on each side, turning once, until fish is golden brown and flakes easily when tested with a fork. (Cooking time will vary depending upon the thickness of the fish.)
7. Drain on paper towels placed over a layer of newspaper or a brown paper bag.
8. Serve with lemon wedges or sauce, if desired (see Chapter 7, Catfish Condiments).

Not Your Daddy's

Hints for Healthy Eating

For many of us, the word "catfish" conjures up an image of platters piled high with fried fish served by sassy waitresses in an all-you-can eat catfish joint. If you are one of the millions of Americans watching their fat intake, you probably haven't been to one of those restaurants in a while and seldom eat much fried food at all. Don't despair—there are recipes in this cookbook for you.

This collection of recipes was compiled with a nod to both tradition and nutrition. While we tried to remain true to the spirit of the original recipes provided by our friends, occasionally we reduced obvious excesses in fat or salt. Listed below are a few things you can do to ensure more nutritious choices.

❦ Select recipes using low-fat preparation techniques. Try grilled, baked, microwaved, poached, and oven-fried catfish.

❦ Use herbs and spices, rather than salt and fat, to provide flavor.

❦ Use a nonstick skillet or spray to reduce or eliminate fat.

❦ Experiment with the recipes if they contain too much fat or salt for your taste.

(Fried) Catfish

When given a choice in a recipe, use low-fat mayonnaise or salad dressing.

Use garlic powder or onion powder instead of seasoned salts. Better yet, use fresh garlic and onion when appropriate.

Use vegetable oils, as suggested in the recipes, instead of melted lard or shortening.

Use a very light hand when the recipe says "salt to taste."

Use restraint when serving yourself tartar sauce or remoulade sauce. Or simply use a squeeze of juice from a fresh lemon or lime.

Follow the Hints for Frying on pages 16–17 (proper oil temperature, fresh oil, draining on paper towels, etc.) to ensure that the catfish you do fry soaks up the least amount of oil.

Notes:

2 Uptown Eating

Catfish Dishes with an International Flair

32   Catfish Piccata
33   Breezy Caribbean Catfish
35   Teriyaki Catfish
36   Tangy Lime-Peppercorn Catfish
37   Athenian Broiled Catfish
38   Tequila-Lime Catfish
39   Catfish Provençal
40   Mexicali Catfish
41   Riviera Catfish

Catfish Piccata

This recipe also works well with chicken fillets or very thin pork chops.

Easy
Serves 2

2 catfish fillets, 4 to 6 ounces each
Salt and pepper to taste

Juice of ½ lemon
1 tablespoon
vegetable oil

Sauce:
Juice of ½ lemon
1 clove garlic, finely minced
1 tablespoon butter or margarine
2 tablespoons white wine
1 tablespoon parsley, minced (optional)
1 tablespoon capers, rinsed (optional)
Lemon slices

1. Rinse catfish under cool, running water and pat dry with paper towels.
2. Season fillets on both sides with salt and pepper. Sprinkle with lemon juice.
3. Heat oil in a heavy skillet over medium heat. Add catfish and sauté for 2 to 4 minutes on each side, turning once. The fish is done when it is no longer translucent at the thickest part and flakes easily when tested with a fork. (Cooking time will vary depending upon the thickness of the fish.)
4. Remove catfish to a warm serving platter.
5. For the sauce, stir lemon juice and minced garlic into drippings. Add butter or margarine. Stir for 1 to 2 minutes.
6. Add wine, parsley, and capers and continue to stir 2 to 3 minutes longer.
7. Spoon lemon-butter-wine sauce over fish and serve. Garnish with lemon slices.

Breezy Caribbean Catfish

This delightfully different recipe can be prepared in less than fifteen minutes.

Easy
Serves 2

2 catfish fillets, 4 to 6 ounces each
Salt and pepper to taste
1 tablespoon vegetable oil

Sauce:
1 tablespoon vegetable oil
2 tablespoons chopped green, red, or yellow onions
½ medium red, yellow, or banana pepper, cut into thin strips
1 clove garlic, minced
½ cup fresh orange juice
½ teaspoon orange zest (grate the orange part of the peel, not the white pith)
1 teaspoon cumin or to taste
Dash of hot pepper sauce or to taste
Orange slices (optional)
2 tablespoons fresh parsley, chopped (optional)

Fascinating Herb & Spice Facts

If you run out of one herb and want to substitute another, a good rule is to experiment within the same family line. For example, the mint family contains basil, marjoram, oregano, rosemary, thyme, and sage. The parsley family contains caraway, chervil, coriander (cilantro), and dill.

1. Rinse catfish under cool, running water and pat dry with paper towels. Salt and pepper both sides.
2. Heat oil in a heavy skillet over medium heat. Add catfish and sauté for 2 to 4 minutes on each side, turning once. The fish is done when it is no longer translucent at the thickest part and flakes easily when tested with a fork. (Cooking time will vary depending upon the thickness of the fish.)
3. Remove catfish to a warm serving platter.
4. For the sauce, add oil to skillet. Sauté onion, pepper, and garlic for 2 to 3 minutes until onion and peppers are limp.
5. Add orange juice, orange zest, cumin, and hot pepper sauce. Simmer for 2 to 3 minutes until juice is reduced by half.
6. Pour orange sauce over catfish. Garnish with orange slices and parsley.

Fascinating Herb & Spice Facts

If you substitute dry for fresh herbs, one teaspoon dried herbs equals 3 teaspoons (one tablespoon) fresh. If you're using garlic, ⅛ teaspoon powdered garlic equals 1 garlic clove.

Though it has the taste of clove, nutmeg, and cinnamon, allspice is not a blend of spices but a dried berry (not a seed) from the pimento tree.

Chili powder, like curry powder, is a blend of spices. Check the label for ingredients such as cayenne, oregano, garlic, salt, and even sugar.

Pepper has been called the king of spices and was once more valuable than gold. Always best fresh ground, it comes in black, white, red, pink, and green. Cayenne pepper is finely ground from the pods of ripe chili peppers.

Teriyaki Catfish

To be safe, don't reuse the marinade for basting. Always reserve part of the marinade in a separate dish to use for basting. This is also delicious cooked on the grill over glowing coals.

Moderately Easy
Serves 4

4 catfish fillets, 4 to 6 ounces each
⅓ cup orange juice
¼ cup low sodium soy sauce
⅓ cup dry, white wine
2 tablespoons vegetable oil
1 tablespoon fresh ginger, grated
1 teaspoon dry mustard
1 teaspoon lemon juice

1 clove garlic, minced
Pinch of sugar
¼ teaspoon black pepper
Cooking spray or
vegetable oil

1. Rinse catfish under cool, running water and pat dry with paper towels.
2. Mix all other ingredients except the oil in a shallow bowl. Reserve 4 tablespoons of marinade in a separate cup.
3. Marinate fillets 15 to 20 minutes in a nonmetallic dish, turning once.
4. Preheat broiler. While fillets are marinating and broiler is heating, simmer reserved marinade in a small pan for 2 to 3 minutes until flavors mix.
5. Remove fish from marinade. Lightly coat broiler pan with cooking spray or vegetable oil. Place fillets in one layer on pan.
6. Broil fillets approximately 4 inches from heat source for 6 to 10 minutes. Baste with reserved, heated marinade. The fish is done when it is no longer translucent at the thickest part and flakes easily when tested with a fork. (Cooking time will vary depending upon the thickness of the fish.)

Tangy Lime-Peppercorn Catfish

This no-salt recipe gets it flavor from spices, lime juice, and freshly ground pepper.

Very Easy
Serves 2

2 catfish fillets, 4 to 6 ounces each
Spices (dried marjoram or oregano, dried thyme, dried parsley, cumin, cayenne pepper, garlic powder)
1 tablespoon vegetable oil

Sauce:
1 tablespoon butter or margarine
⅓ cup fresh lime juice
Freshly ground black pepper
1 teaspoon fresh lime segments (optional)

1. Rinse catfish under cool, running water and pat dry with paper towels.
2. Sprinkle fillets on both sides with a combination of spices of your choice. Your own taste will guide you as to how heavily to use spices.
3. Heat oil in a heavy skillet over medium heat. Add catfish and sauté for 2 to 4 minutes on each side, turning once. The fish is done when it is no longer translucent at the thickest part and flakes easily when tested with a fork. (Cooking time will vary depending upon the thickness of the fish.)
4. Remove catfish to a warm serving platter.
5. For the sauce, add butter or margarine and lime juice to skillet and stir to blend pan juices. When heated, grind fresh black pepper to taste over sauce. Add lime segments, if desired , and pour hot sauce over fillets.

Athenian Broiled Catfish

This is based on a recipe by Sophia Clikas, a wonderful cook from Mobile, Alabama. Serve with a Greek salad, some crusty bread, and retsina wine. Perfect!

Very Easy
Serves 4

4 catfish fillets, 4 to 6 ounces each
Cooking spray or vegetable oil
2 tablespoons butter or margarine, melted
Salt and pepper to taste

Sauce:
Juice of one lemon
1 teaspoon dried oregano
2 tablespoons butter or margarine, melted
2 tablespoons parsley, minced (optional)
Lemon slices (optional)

1. Preheat broiler.
2. Rinse catfish under cool, running water and pat dry with paper towels.
3. Lightly coat broiler pan with cooking spray or vegetable oil. Place fish in one layer on broiler pan and replace under broiler.
4. Melt butter or margarine in a small saucepan. Brush fish with melted butter. Sprinkle lightly with salt and pepper.
5. Broil fish approximately 4 inches away from heat source for about 6 to 10 minutes. Fish is done when it is no longer translucent at the thickest part and flakes easily when tested with a fork. (Cooking time will vary depending upon the thickness of the fish.)
6. Remove catfish to a warm serving platter.
7. For the sauce, whisk the lemon juice and oregano into remaining butter or margarine.
8. Pour sauce over fillets. Sprinkle with parsley and serve with lemon slices, if desired.

Tequila-Lime Catfish

This inventive recipe conjures up visions of Mexico, sunshine, and salt air.

> *Very Easy*
> *Serves 4*
>
> 4 catfish fillets, 4 to 6 ounces each
> ½ cup bread crumbs
> Salt and pepper to taste
> 2 tablespoons vegetable oil or margarine
>
> *Sauce:*
> 3 tablespoons tequila
> Juice of 1 lime
> Lime slices (optional)
> Parsley (optional)

1. Rinse catfish under cool, running water and pat dry with paper towels.
2. Dredge fish in bread crumbs seasoned with salt and pepper.
3. Heat oil or melt margarine in a heavy skillet over medium heat.
4. Add catfish and sauté for 2 to 4 minutes on each side, turning once. The fish is done when it is no longer translucent at the thickest part and flakes easily when tested with a fork. (Cooking time will vary depending upon the thickness of the fish.)
5. Remove catfish to a warm serving platter.
6. For the sauce, add tequila and lime juice to skillet and cook an additional minute. Pour mixture over fish before serving. May be garnished with lime slices and chopped parsley, if desired.

Catfish Provençal

The wonderful aromas of garlic and olive oil flavor this dish. Use crusty French bread to dip in the sauce.

Very Easy
Serves 2

2 catfish fillets, 4 to 6 ounces each
Juice of 1 lemon
Salt and pepper to taste
Olive oil for cooking

Sauce:
1 tablespoon olive oil
2 teaspoons garlic, minced
2 teaspoons jalapeno pepper (or chili peppers), minced

1. Rinse catfish under cool, running water and pat dry with paper towels.
2. Drizzle fish with juice of lemon. Sprinkle with salt and pepper.
3. Add enough oil to a heavy skillet to coat the bottom of the pan.
4. Add catfish to hot pan; reduce to medium heat. Sauté for 2 to 4 minutes on each side, turning once. Fish is done when it is no longer translucent at the thickest part and flakes easily when tested with a fork. (Cooking time will vary depending upon the thickness of the fish.)
5. Remove fish to a warm serving platter.
6. For the sauce, add 1 tablespoon of olive oil to the skillet. Add garlic and peppers and cook for 1 to 2 minutes until garlic is translucent. Stir pan juices and the oil. Do not overcook. Pour hot sauce over fish (see Chapter 9, Foreign Friends, for companion salads or side dishes).

Mexicali Catfish

For instant tortilla crumbs, place chips in a plastic baggie, press out the air, seal the bag, then crush with a rolling pin. If a rolling pin isn't handy, use a wine or soft drink bottle.

Easy
Serves 4

Vegetable oil or cooking spray
1 cup tortilla chips, finely crushed
½ teaspoon cumin
½ teaspoon chili powder
2 tablespoons lime juice
2 tablespoon vegetable oil
4 catfish fillets, 4 to 6 ounces each
1 cup salsa (See Chapter 7, Catfish Condiments, for salsa recipe.)
Chopped cilantro (optional)

1. Preheat oven to 400°.
2. Coat a baking sheet with vegetable oil or cooking spray.
3. Mix finely crushed tortilla chips, cumin, and chili powder in a shallow bowl or pie pan.
4. Mix lime juice and oil in a nonmetallic shallow bowl.
5. Rinse catfish under cool, running water and pat dry with paper towels.
6. Dip catfish in lime juice mix, then dredge in tortilla chip mixture. Coat well.
7. Place in one layer on baking sheet. Bake for 10 to 20 minutes or until fish is no longer translucent at the thickest part and flakes easily when tested with a fork. (Cooking time will vary depending upon the thickness of the fish.)
8. As fish is baking, warm the salsa in a small pan over low heat.
9. Remove fish from the oven. Arrange the fillets on plates and spoon salsa over fish. Garnish with fresh chopped cilantro, if desired.

Riviera Catfish

If fresh herbs aren't available, 1½ to 2 teaspoons of dried Italian herbs are a good substitute. Try any mixture of the following: basil, bay leaf, marjoram, oregano, parsley, savory, and thyme.

Easy
Serves 4

4 catfish fillets, 4 to 6 ounces each
⅓ cup fresh lemon juice
2 tablespoons olive oil
1 medium onion, chopped
1 red or green pepper, seeded and chopped
1 clove garlic, minced
2 tomatoes, peeled, seeded, and chopped
½ tablespoon fresh sage, chopped
1 tablespoon fresh basil, chopped
Salt and pepper to taste
Cooking spray or olive oil
½ cup Parmesan cheese, grated
Fresh basil or sage (optional)

Fascinating Herb Facts

Coriander is one of the world's most widely used culinary herbs. Fresh coriander is known as cilantro or Chinese parsley. Dried coriander is made from the seeds of coriander (Coriander sativum).

Most herbs can be used fresh or dried. Chives, best cut fresh from the garden, may be an exception. Small bunches of leafy herbs can be dried in a dark room. Tie the stems in small bunches and hang them upside down in a room with low humidity. In summer, they should dry in about two weeks.

1. Preheat oven to 400°.
2. Rinse catfish under cool, running water and pat dry with paper towels. Marinate fillets in lemon juice for 15 minutes in a non-metallic dish.
3. Heat olive oil in a preheated heavy skillet, and sauté onion, pepper, and garlic until onion becomes translucent (about 3 minutes). Add tomatoes and cook for 2 to 3 minutes longer.
4. Add sage, basil, salt, and pepper and stir for 30 seconds. Set aside.
5. Lightly coat baking dish with cooking spray or olive oil. Remove fish from marinade and place in baking dish. Spoon vegetable-herb sauce over each fillet.
6. Bake uncovered for 10 to 20 minutes or until fish is no longer translucent at the thickest part and flakes easily when tested with a fork. (Cooking time will vary depending upon the thickness of the fish.)
7. Sprinkle cheese over fish and bake 2 to 3 minutes longer or until cheese melts.
8. Garnish with fresh basil or sage, if desired.

3 Up-a-Lazy-River Recipes

Microwaving, Grilling, and Poaching Catfish the Easy Way

Hints for Microwaving, Grilling, and Poaching Catfish   44
Polynesian Catfish   45
Ginger-Garlic Catfish   46
Rosemary Catfish   47
Incredibly Easy Breaded Catfish   48
Catfish Isabella   49
Oriental Grilled Catfish   50
Lemon-Basil Grilled Catfish   51
Easy Italian Grilled Catfish   52
Easy Poached Catfish   53
The Literary and Lyrical Catfish—   54
Memorialized in Story and Song

Hints for Microwaving Catfish

❦ Cut fish into serving-size pieces before microwaving.
❦ Use high-power setting.
❦ Microwave 3 to 5 minutes per pound.
❦ Use a shallow dish.
❦ Cover with lid or plastic wrap, one corner vented to let steam escape.
❦ Rotate dish one-quarter turn when half through cooking process if you do not have a turntable in your microwave. Check for doneness at this time.
❦ Let food stand 2 to 3 minutes before serving.

Hints for Grilling Catfish

❦ Cut fish into serving-size pieces before grilling unless you're grilling a whole fish.
❦ Avoid using treated briquettes or lighter fluid to start the fire. Fish can easily pick up unwanted flavors.
❦ Always brush the grill or grill pan with oil before it heats up.
❦ Marinate fish before cooking and/or baste during grilling.
❦ Prepare two sets of marinade—one as marinade for the fish and one for basting. Discard the first after removing the fish.
❦ Use medium-hot coals that are ash gray, occasionally glowing red.
❦ Use "flavored" woods, such as mesquite or cherry, for extra flavor or throw your favorite herbs on the fire. Sprigs of rosemary, thyme, or oregano soaked for 30 minutes in cold water work well.

Hints for Poaching Catfish

❦ Wait until after poaching to cut fish or large fillets into smaller portions.
❦ Use just enough liquid to cover the catfish.
❦ Heat the liquid to simmering, then add the fish.
❦ Do not boil the fish.
❦ Cook 10 minutes per inch of thickness.
❦ Check fish often for doneness so it does not overcook.
❦ Reduce liquid and boil down for sauce after fish is removed.

Polynesian Catfish (microwave)

Dark, not light, sesame oil is used in this recipe to provide a delicious, nutty flavor.

Easy
Serves 4

1 tablespoon dark sesame oil
2 tablespoons soy sauce
2 tablespoons fresh lemon juice
1 teaspoon fresh ginger, grated
¼ teaspoon red pepper flakes
1 teaspoon garlic, minced
4 catfish fillets, 4 to 6 ounces each
½ green pepper, diced
½ red bell pepper, diced
½ cup pineapple tidbits, drained
Sliced green onions
4 cups cooked rice

1. Combine first 6 ingredients in a small bowl.
2. Rinse catfish under cool, running water and pat dry with paper towels.
3. Place fish in one layer in a microwave-safe dish. Tuck under any thin sections so the fish is an even thickness.
4. Sprinkle green and red peppers and pineapple bits over fish. Pour sesame oil mix over all.
5. Cover with lid or plastic wrap, leaving one corner vented to allow steam to escape. Microwave on high for approximately 5 minutes or until fish is no longer translucent at the thickest part and flakes easily when tested with a fork. If you do not have a turntable in your microwave oven, give the dish a quarter turn after 2½ minutes. Let catfish stand for 2 to 3 minutes before serving.
6. Sprinkle fish with green onions and serve over rice.

Ginger-Garlic Catfish (microwave)

Hoisin sauce, a sweet, soy-based condiment used in Chinese cooking, is readily found in most supermarkets.

Easy
Serves 4

2 tablespoons dark sesame oil
1 tablespoon soy sauce
1 tablespoon hoisin sauce
2 tablespoons dry sherry
2 teaspoons fresh ginger, grated
¼ teaspoon red pepper flakes
1 teaspoon garlic, minced
4 catfish fillets, 4-6 ounces each
Sliced green onions
4 cups cooked rice

1. Combine first 7 ingredients in a small bowl.
2. Rinse catfish under cool, running water and pat dry with paper towels.
3. Place fish in one layer in a microwave-safe dish. Tuck under any thin sections so fish is an even thickness.
4. Pour sesame oil mix over the fish.
5. Cover with lid or plastic wrap, leaving one corner vented to allow steam to escape. Microwave on high for approximately 5 minutes or until fish is no longer translucent at the thickest part and flakes easily when tested with a fork. If you do not have a turntable in your microwave oven, give the dish a quarter turn after 2½ minutes. Let fish stand for 2 to 3 minutes before serving.
6. Sprinkle fish with green onions and serve over rice.

Rosemary Catfish (microwave)

Dried herbs can be used, but fresh rosemary and parsley really make this recipe sing of hot summer days on the Riviera.

Very Easy
Serves 4

2 tablespoons olive oil
1 tablespoon fresh lemon juice
2 tablespoons white wine
4 catfish fillets, 4 to 6 ounces each
Salt and pepper to taste
4 to 6 sprigs fresh rosemary
1 tablespoon fresh parsley, chopped

1. In a small, nonmetallic bowl, blend olive oil, lemon juice, and wine.
2. Rinse catfish under cool, running water and pat dry with paper towels. Sprinkle both sides of fish with salt and pepper.
3. Place fish in one layer in a microwave-safe dish. Tuck under any thin sections so fish is an even thickness.
4. Pour sauce over fish, and arrange rosemary sprigs on top of fish.
5. Cover with lid or plastic wrap, leaving one corner vented to allow steam to escape. Microwave on high for approximately 5 minutes or until fish is no longer translucent at the thickest part and flakes easily when tested with a fork. If you do not have a turntable in your microwave oven, give the dish a quarter turn after 2½ minutes. Let fish stand for 2 to 3 minutes before serving. Garnish with parsley.

Incredibly Easy Breaded Catfish (microwave)

Low-fat Italian dressing can be substituted in this recipe. From start to finish, this easy dish takes less than 15 minutes.

Very Easy
Serves 2

⅓ cup Italian dressing
½ cup seasoned breadcrumbs
2 catfish fillets, 4 to 6 ounces each
Cooking spray
Paprika
Sliced green onions
Lemon wedges

1. Pour dressing into a shallow bowl.
2. Put seasoned breadcrumbs in a separate shallow bowl or pie pan.
3. Rinse catfish under cool, running water and pat dry with paper towels.
4. Spray microwave-safe dish with cooking spray.
5. Dip fillets first in salad dressing, then dredge in breadcrumbs. Coat well. Sprinkle with paprika.
6. Place fish in one layer in a microwave-safe dish. Tuck under any thin sections so fish is an even thickness.
7. Cover with lid or plastic wrap, leaving one corner vented to allow steam to escape. Microwave on high for approximately 5 minutes or until fish is no longer translucent at the thickest part and flakes easily when tested with a fork. If you do not have a turntable in your microwave oven, give the dish a quarter turn after 2½ minutes. Let fish stand for 2 to 3 minutes before serving.
8. Sprinkle with sliced green onions and serve with lemon wedges.

Catfish Isabella (microwave)

Spanish olives give this elegant dish a Mediterranean flair.

Easy
Serves 2

2 catfish fillets, 4 to 6 ounces each
Juice of fresh lime
2 ripe tomatoes, peeled and
chopped
3 to 4 green onions, chopped
1 jalapeno pepper, seeded
and minced
1 bay leaf
2 tablespoons Spanish olives, chopped

2 garlic cloves, minced
½ tablespoon olive oil
⅓ cup water
Salt and pepper to taste

1. Rinse catfish under cool, running water and pat dry with paper towels. Marinate in fresh lime juice in a nonmetallic dish for 15 minutes, turning once.
2. Mix next 8 ingredients in a microwave-safe dish. Cover with lid or plastic wrap, leaving one corner vented to allow steam to escape. Cook on high for about 5 minutes, then let stand covered 2 to 3 minutes covered.
3. Salt and pepper catfish on both sides. Place fillets in one layer in a microwave-safe dish. Tuck under any thin sections so the fish is an even thickness. Pour sauce over fish.
4. Cover loosely with wax paper. Microwave on high for approximately 5 minutes or until fish is no longer translucent at the thickest part and flakes easily when tested with a fork. If you do not have a turntable in your microwave oven, give the dish a quarter turn after 2½ minutes and check for doneness. Let fish stand for 2 to 3 minutes after removing from the microwave.

Hint: Use canned jalapeno peppers. One canned pepper equals approximately 1 tablespoon of minced fresh pepper.

Oriental Grilled Catfish

This simple catfish dish has a wonderfully exotic taste.

Easy
Serves 4 to 6

4 to 6 catfish fillets, 4 to 6 ounces each
2 tablespoons dark sesame oil
¼ cup soy sauce
3 tablespoons fresh lemon juice
1 tablespoon fresh ginger, grated
l clove garlic, sliced
Pepper to taste
Cooking spray or vegetable oil
Sliced green onions (optional)

1. Rinse catfish under cool, running water and pat dry with paper towels.
2. Combine next 6 ingredients in shallow, nonmetallic dish. Reserve 2 to 3 tablespoons for basting. Add catfish to marinade and coat both sides.
3. Cover and marinate in refrigerator for about 30 minutes, turning fish occasionally.
4. Lightly coat grill or grill basket with cooking spray or vegetable oil.
5. Heat grill to medium-hot (heating times vary for different grills). The coals should be ash gray, occasionally glowing red.
6. Discard marinade. Grill fish about 3 to 5 minutes on each side or until fish is no longer translucent at the thickest part and flakes easily when tested with a fork. (Cooking time will vary depending upon the thickness of the fish.)
7. Baste with reserved marinade, checking often so that fish does not overcook.
8. Garnish with green onions, if desired.

Lemon-Basil Grilled Catfish

Basil is easy to grow in your garden or in a pot on the patio. Always have some fresh basil on hand.

> *Easy*
> *Serves 4 to 6*
>
> 4 to 6 catfish fillets, 4 to 6 ounces each
> ½ cup fresh lemon juice (or dry white wine)
> ½ cup vegetable oil
> 1 teaspoon hot pepper sauce
> ½ teaspoon salt
> 1 tablespoon fresh basil
> Cooking spray or vegetable oil
> Sprigs of fresh basil (optional)

1. Rinse catfish under cool, running water and pat dry with paper towels.
2. Combine next 5 ingredients in shallow, nonmetallic dish. Reserve 2 to 3 tablespoons for basting. Add catfish to marinade and coat both sides.
3. Cover and marinate catfish in refrigerator for about 30 minutes, turning fish occasionally.
4. Lightly coat grill or grill basket with cooking spray or vegetable oil.
5. Heat grill to medium-hot (heating times vary for different grills). The coals should be ash gray, occasionally glowing red.
6. Discard marinade, and grill fish about 3 to 5 minutes on each side or until fish is no longer translucent at the thickest part and flakes easily when tested with a fork. (Cooking time will vary depending upon the thickness of the fish.)
7. Baste with reserved marinade, checking often so that fish does not overcook.
8. Garnish with sprigs of fresh basil, if desired.

Easy Italian Grilled Catfish

Either low-fat or regular dressing works in this recipe.

Very Easy
Serves 4 to 6

4 to 6 catfish fillets, 4 to 6 ounces each
1 cup commercially prepared Italian dressing
2 tablespoons fresh lemon juice
Cooking spray or vegetable oil
Lemon slices (optional)

1. Rinse catfish under cool, running water and pat dry with paper towels.
2. Combine dressing and lemon juice in a shallow, nonmetallic dish. Reserve 2 to 3 tablespoons for basting. Add catfish to marinade and coat both sides.
3. Cover and marinate catfish in refrigerator for about 30 minutes, turning fish occasionally.
4. Lightly coat grill or grill basket with cooking spray or vegetable oil.
5. Heat grill to medium-hot (heating times vary for different grills). The coals should be ash gray, occasionally glowing red.
6. Discard marinade and grill fish about 3 to 5 minutes on each side or until fish is no longer translucent at the thickest part and flakes easily when tested with a fork. (Cooking time will vary depending upon the thickness of the fish.)
7. Baste with reserved marinade, checking often so that fish does not overcook.
8. Garnish with lemon slices, if desired.

Easy Poached Catfish

This is a low-calorie, low-fat recipe.

Very Easy
Serves 2

    2 cups water (may include ½ cup white wine)
    2 to 3 tablespoons lemon juice
    1 small onion, sliced
    ½ teaspoon salt
    2 teaspoons peppercorns
    1 bay leaf
    2 to 3 sprigs fresh parsley and/or thyme
    2 catfish fillets, 4 to 6 ounces each
    Lemon, thinly sliced
    Sauce (optional)

1. Combine water, lemon juice, onion, salt, peppercorns, bay leaf, and parsley and/or thyme in a heavy skillet. Bring to a boil. Let simmer 3 to 5 minutes so flavors merge.
2. Rinse catfish under cool, running water and pat dry with paper towels.
3. Adjust the heat so the fish does not boil. Place the fish in the liquid. If liquid doesn't cover the fish, turn the fish once while cooking.
4. Simmer 10 minutes per inch of thickness. Fish is done when it is no longer translucent at the thickest part and flakes easily when tested with a fork. Check often so fish does not overcook. Hint: Drain and save liquid for fish stock.
5. Use a wide spatula to remove fish carefully from liquid. If desired, serve with lemon slices and sauce, such as Low-fat Horseradish or Yogurt-Mint Sauce (see Chapter 7, Catfish Condiments).

The Literary

Memorialized in Story and Song

What other fish is so lovingly memorialized in story and song? Not tuna, grouper, bass, cod, flounder, whitefish, or salmon.

In the past, world-renowned authors, such as Nobel Prize winner William Faulkner, celebrated catfish. Faulkner used one of America's most famous catfish eateries, Taylor's Groceries and Restaurant in Taylor, Mississippi, as a setting in his novel *Sanctuary*, published in 1931. Present-day writers John Grisham and Willie Morris often stop by Taylor's to sample fried catfish and hushpuppies. And, of course, both DuBose Heyward and George Gershwin immortalized Charleston's Catfish Row as the setting where Porgy and Bess loved and lost.

Recently, James Lee Burke began his novel *Sunset Limited*, set in Louisiana, with a vignette of catfish fishing. The author even described a character as having a mouth that curved like a catfish. Margaret Maron, the North Carolina mystery writer, sent one of her characters catfishing on Possum Creek in her 1998 novel, *Home Fires*. And further north, in Seattle, Washington, Earl Emerson called his 1998 mystery, *Catfish Cafe*.

and Lyrical Catfish

In *Little Altars Everywhere*, Rebecca Wells devotes a chapter to "Catfish Dreams," in which the town of Thornton, Louisiana, pins its hopes for revitalization on turning the city swimming pool into a catfish farm. One of the characters tells a story about a cousin who caught a catfish as big as a car. And in keeping with the fantastic, T. Coraghessan Boyle, in *The Tortilla Curtain*, describes roads in Florida disappearing under masses of Siamese walking catfish waddling from one canal to the next.

Modern poet Richard Brautigan wrote a romantic ode about whiskers, wrinkled skin, and the moon, "Your Catfish Friend." Not so romantic is John Charles McNeil's four-line poem, "Possum Time," in which he compares the delights of tough and tender catfish to possum! And five hundred years earlier, over thirty poems were written by Zen Buddhist priests to a catfish in a painting. The enigmatic *Catching a Catfish with a Gourd*, along with the poems, hangs in the National Museum in Kyota, Japan.

Catfish have not been neglected in the musical world. The Grateful Dead gave us "Catfish John"; Jimi Hendrix, "Catfish Blues"; Larry Johnson, simply "Catfish"; and Jethro Tull, the album *Catfish Rising*. And the Moody Blues croon that catfish are jumpin' in "Blackwater."

Although he wasn't a writer, North Carolina's Jim "Catfish" Hunter was a poet on the baseball field when he pitched a perfect game in 1986.

Notes:

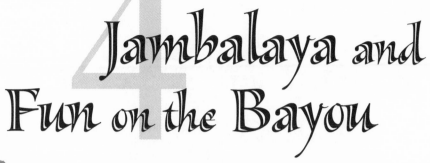

Jambalaya and Fun on the Bayou

Cajun and Creole Cuisine

58 *Cajun and Creole Cooking*

59 Catfish Gumbo

60 *Keeping Catfish Fresh and Sassy—*
    Hints for Buying and Storing Catfish

61 Catfish with Remoulade Sauce

62 Catfish Jambalaya

63 Creole Catfish

64 Blackened Catfish

Cajun and Creole Cooking

Fabulous food is part of the heritage of Louisiana, bringing together two great cultures—Cajun and Creole.

The Cajuns are descended from farmers from the south of France who first emigrated to Nova Scotia. As we remember from Longfellow's poem "Evangeline," they were driven from Canada by the British in the 1700s and made the long, arduous trek to the bayous of Louisiana. The Acadians, or Cajuns, were farmers, trappers, and hunters who made use of the ingredients they found in their new home—fish and crayfish, hot peppers, rice, bay leaves, okra brought from Africa by slaves, and filé powder, ground leaves of the sassafras tree, provided by the Choctaw Indians. Cajun food began as hearty, spicy country fare.

Meanwhile, in New Orleans, other cultures were merging and inventing a new Creole cuisine. Distinctive French, Spanish, and Italian cooking styles, with a strong influence from the shores of Africa, were adapted and changed into recipes served in the finest homes and restaurants. In the early days, seven different flags flew over Louisiana, and each nation made its own contribution to Creole cooking. Today the line may be blurred between Cajun and Creole cuisine, but no matter the recipe's origin, the results will be special.

Catfish Gumbo

This is a quick and easy gumbo, ready in about an hour from start to finish. Serve with hot, crusty bread for a satisfying meal.

Moderately Easy
Serves 4 to 6

2 tablespoons vegetable oil or olive oil
1 cup onion, chopped
1 cup celery, chopped
1 cup green pepper, chopped
2 cloves garlic, minced
4 cups fish, vegetable, or chicken stock
14.5-ounce can diced tomatoes with juice
1 teaspoon dried thyme
1 teaspoon dried oregano
½ teaspoon cayenne pepper
½ teaspoon hot pepper sauce
1 teaspoon salt
1 bay leaf
10-ounce package frozen, sliced okra
1 pound catfish, about 3 fillets
¾ pound shrimp, peeled and deveined
4 cups cooked rice

1. Heat oil in a heavy pot over medium heat. Sauté onion, celery, green pepper, and garlic until vegetables become translucent.
2. Stir in stock, tomatoes, spices, and herbs. Bring to a boil, then cover and simmer for 15 to 20 minutes.
3. Add okra and cook the amount of time recommended on the package.

4. Rinse catfish under cool, running water and pat dry with paper towels. Cut into 1- to 2-inch cubes. Add catfish and cook for 5 to 8 minutes.
5. Add shrimp and cook for 2 to 3 minutes longer.
6. Remove bay leaf. Serve over rice.

Keeping Catfish Fresh and Sassy

Hints for Buying and Storing Catfish

❝ Buy the freshest catfish available. The fish should smell fresh and clean; the skin should be firm, moist, and translucent. The flesh should be springy to the touch, and if the head is on the fish, the eyes should be bright and clear.

❝ Store the fish in its original wrapping in the refrigerator for 24 hours only. Put the fish in the coldest part of the refrigerator.

❝ Rinse the fish under cool, running water before you prepare it for cooking. Pat dry with paper towels.

❝ Freeze the fish by rinsing it, patting it dry with paper towels, then wrapping it in plastic wrap and then in aluminum foil or a sealed plastic bag. Remember to date your bag. You may freeze catfish up to 4 months.

❝ Wash your hands with hot water and soap before and after handling any type of fish.

❝ Thaw catfish in the refrigerator. Place the wrapped fish in a leak-proof container for thawing overnight or throughout the day.

❝ Speed thawing by placing wrapped, frozen catfish in the sink under cool, running water.

Catfish with Remoulade Sauce

To make this easy recipe even easier, use bagged, commercially prepared greens from your produce section.

Very Easy
Serves 2

2 cups of mixed greens (Try arugula, romaine, Bibb lettuce, escarole, and radicchio.)
2 catfish fillets, 4 to 6 ounces each, sliced in half lengthwise
Salt and pepper to taste
1 teaspoon paprika
2 tablespoons butter or margarine
1 cup remoulade sauce (see Chapter 7, Catfish Condiments)
Lemon slices

1. Arrange one cup of greens on each plate.
2. Rinse catfish under cool, running water and pat dry with paper towels.
3. Sprinkle catfish on both sides with salt, pepper, and paprika.
4. Melt butter or margarine in a heavy skillet over medium heat. Sauté catfish for 2 to 4 minutes on each side, turning once, until fish is no longer translucent at the thickest part and flakes easily when tested with a fork. (Cooking time will vary depending upon the thickness of the fish.)
5. Place catfish in an X formation across the greens. Top each plate with ½ cup of remoulade sauce or serve sauce on the side.
6. Garnish with lemon slices.

Catfish Jambalaya

You'll have fun on the bayou with this easy Cajun dish.

Moderately Easy
Serves 6 to 8

2 tablespoons vegetable oil
2 cups onion, chopped
1 cup celery, chopped
1 cup green peppers, chopped
3 cloves garlic, minced
2 14.5-ounce cans diced tomatoes with juice
2 bay leaves
2 cups fish or chicken stock
1 cup uncooked rice
1 pound catfish, cut into 1-inch cubes
¾ pound turkey ham, cut into 1-inch cubes
Salt and pepper to taste
Hot pepper sauce (optional)

1. Heat oil in a heavy pot over medium heat. Sauté onions, celery, green peppers, and garlic until vegetables become translucent.
2. Add tomatoes and bay leaves. Simmer uncovered 5 minutes.
3. Add stock and rice. Bring to a boil while stirring. Reduce heat to simmer; cover and cook for 10 minutes.
4. Add catfish and turkey ham. Cook covered for an additional 10 minutes or until the rice is tender but firm and fish flakes easily when tested with a fork.
5. Add salt, pepper, and hot sauce to taste. Remove bay leaves.

Creole Catfish

This is an easy-bake dish, once again using the holy trinity of Creole and Cajun cooking: onion, celery, and green pepper.

Easy
Serves 4

1 tablespoon vegetable oil
½ cup onion, chopped
½ cup celery, chopped
½ cup green pepper, chopped
14.5-ounce can diced tomatoes
¼ cup tomato paste
½ teaspoon dried or 1½ teaspoons fresh basil
4 catfish fillets, 4 to 6 ounces each
Cooking spray or vegetable oil
Salt and pepper to taste
4 cups cooked rice

1. Preheat oven to 400°.
2. Heat oil in a heavy skillet over medium heat. Sauté onion, celery, and green pepper until vegetables become translucent.
3. Add tomatoes, tomato paste, and basil. Simmer 5 minutes.
4. While sauce is simmering, rinse catfish under cool, running water and pat dry with paper towels. Place fillets in one layer in a baking dish that has been lightly coated with cooking spray or vegetable oil.
5. Taste sauce and adjust seasonings. Add salt and pepper to taste. Pour sauce over fillets.
6. Bake for 10 to 20 minutes or until fish is no longer translucent at the thickest part and flakes easily when tested with a fork. (Cooking time will vary depending upon the thickness of the fish.)
7. Serve with rice.

Blackened Catfish

This is a New Orleans favorite with many variations. Try this one, then experiment on your own.

Easy
Serves 4

1 tablespoon paprika
2 teaspoons dried basil
1½ teaspoons garlic powder
1½ teaspoons black pepper
1½ teaspoons sugar
1 teaspoon cayenne pepper or to taste
1 teaspoon dried thyme
½ teaspoon salt
4 catfish fillets, 4 to 6 ounces each
2 tablespoons butter or margarine
Lemon wedges

1. Combine all dry ingredients and spread evenly over a piece of waxed paper.
2. Rinse catfish under cool, running water and pat dry with paper towels.
3. Liberally coat both sides of catfish fillets with spice mixture.
4. Melt butter or margarine in an iron skillet over moderately high heat.
5. Add fillets to hot skillet and cook 2 to 4 minutes on each side, turning once, until fish is no longer translucent at the thickest part and flakes easily when tested with a fork. (Cooking time will vary depending upon the thickness of the fish.)
6. Serve with lemon wedges.

5 A Baker's Half-Dozen

Six Easy-Bake Recipes

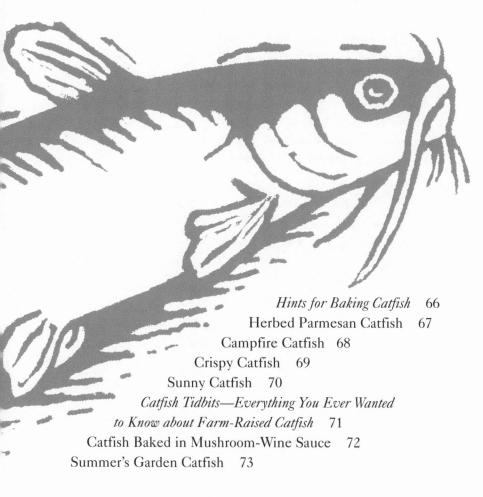

Hints for Baking Catfish   66

Herbed Parmesan Catfish   67

Campfire Catfish   68

Crispy Catfish   69

Sunny Catfish   70

Catfish Tidbits—Everything You Ever Wanted
to Know about Farm-Raised Catfish   71

Catfish Baked in Mushroom-Wine Sauce   72

Summer's Garden Catfish   73

Hints for Baking Catfish

1. Cut fish into serving-size pieces before cooking (unless a whole fish is used). Always rinse fish under cool, running water and pat dry with paper towels. When placing fillets in a baking dish, you may turn thin edges under so fish will cook more evenly.

2. Flaking is the major test for doneness no matter how long the fish is cooked. It should flake easily when tested with a fork. Properly cooked fish is opaque, not translucent. Cook 10 minutes per pound or 10 minutes for each 1 inch of thickness.

3. One of the greatest challenges when baking fish is preventing dryness. Sauces and other coatings help keep the fish moist and flavorful. Fish may also be basted during cooking to discourage drying. Turning the fish isn't necessary, but if you do so, use wide spatulas so the fish does not break up.

4. Test for doneness often. Remember that different stoves set at the same temperature may actually cook at varying temperatures.

Herbed Parmesan Catfish

There are many variations of this recipe, but this one, recommended by Ann Wooten of Atlanta, is both easy and good.

Easy
Serves 4

⅔ cup Parmesan cheese, freshly grated
¼ cup all-purpose flour
½ teaspoon salt
¼ teaspoon pepper
½ teaspoon dried oregano
½ teaspoon dried thyme
1 teaspoon paprika
1 egg, beaten
¼ cup milk
4 catfish fillets, 4 to 6 ounces each
Cooking spray or vegetable oil
2 tablespoons melted butter or margarine
Fresh parsley sprigs (optional)

1. Preheat oven to 400°. Mix first 7 ingredients in a shallow bowl or pie pan.
2. Whisk egg and milk in another shallow bowl.
3. Rinse catfish under cool, running water and pat dry with paper towels.
4. Dip fillets into egg mix, then dredge in cheese/flour mix. Pat down dry mix so it clings to fish.
5. Place fillets in one layer in a baking dish lightly coated with cooking spray or vegetable oil, and drizzle fillets with melted butter or margarine.
6. Bake for 10 to 20 minutes or until fish is no longer translucent at the thickest part and flakes easily when tested with a fork. (Cooking time will vary depending upon the thickness of the fish.)
7. Garnish with fresh parsley, if desired.

Campfire Catfish

Easy preparation and cleanup make this dish great at home or on a camping trip, cooked over hot coals.

Very Easy
Serves as many as you want

Aluminum foil
Cooking spray or vegetable oil
Tomato, sliced
Onion, sliced
Green and/or yellow peppers, sliced
Bottled ranch dressing (or any creamy, prepared dressing)
Italian seasonings (or seasonings of choice such as thyme, oregano, garlic)
Salt and pepper to taste
Any number of catfish fillets
Chives (optional)

1. Preheat oven to 400°. Tear off a 12-by-15-inch piece of aluminum foil for each fillet. Place foil shiny side down on the counter. Lightly coat the dull side with cooking spray or vegetable oil.
2. Rinse catfish under cool, running water and pat dry with paper towels. Place one fillet lengthwise on each piece of greased foil. On each fillet, arrange several slices of tomato, onion, and pepper. Sprinkle with spices, salt, and pepper. Top with a tablespoon of dressing.
3. Seal foil carefully, crimping the ends and sides together to make a packet. Be sure to leave enough room inside the packet for expansion.
4. Bake for 10 minutes. Remove packets from the oven and let stand for 3 to 5 minutes longer. The fish will continue to cook.
5. Open each packet carefully and serve. Sprinkle with chopped chives, if desired.

Crispy Catfish

Alice Enright of Atlanta, who suggested this recipe, says either corn-bread or herb stuffing works great.

Moderately Easy
Serves 4

½ cup bottled Italian dressing
¼ cup fresh lemon juice
4 catfish fillets, 4 to 6 ounces each
½ cup Parmesan cheese, freshly grated
1 cup cornbread or herb stuffing
1½ teaspoons paprika
2 tablespoons fresh parsley, chopped, or 2 teaspoons dried
¼ teaspoon salt
¼ teaspoon pepper

Cooking spray or vegetable oil
2 tablespoons melted butter or margarine
Lemon slices
Fresh parsley sprigs (optional)

1. Preheat oven to 400°. Combine Italian dressing and lemon juice in a shallow, non-metallic dish large enough for 4 fillets.
2. Rinse catfish under cool, running water and pat dry with paper towels. Place in dressing/lemon marinade while preparing dry ingredients. Turn once so both sides are coated with marinade.
3. Mix cheese, stuffing, paprika, chopped parsley, salt, and pepper in another shallow bowl or pie pan.
4. Dredge fillets in cornbread/cheese mix. Pat dry mixture into fish so it clings. Place fillets in one layer in a baking dish lightly coated with cooking spray or vegetable oil. Drizzle fillets with melted butter or margarine.
5. Bake for 10 to 20 minutes or until fish is no longer translucent at the thickest part and flakes easily when tested with a fork. (Cooking time will vary depending upon the thickness of the fish.)
6. Garnish with lemon slices and sprigs of fresh parsley, if desired.

Sunny Catfish

If you feel inventive, mix sesame seeds with the sunflower seeds for a range of tastes and textures.

Easy
Serves 2

2 tablespoons sunflower seeds
1 tablespoon bread crumbs
⅛ teaspoon cayenne pepper or to taste
¼ teaspoon garlic powder or to taste
½ teaspoon paprika
2 tablespoons mayonnaise (regular or low-fat)
1 teaspoon prepared mustard (Dijon or regular)
4 catfish fillets, 4 to 6 ounces each
Salt and pepper to taste
Cooking spray or vegetable oil
Orange slices (optional)

1. Preheat oven to 400°.
2. Mix the first five dry ingredients in a shallow bowl or pie pan
3. In another shallow bowl, mix together mayonnaise and mustard.
4. Rinse catfish under cool, running water and pat dry with paper towels. Salt and pepper each side.
5. Coat fillets with mayonnaise/mustard mix, then dredge in dry ingredients.
6. Place fillets in one layer in a baking dish lightly coated with cooking spray or vegetable oil. Bake for 10 to 20 minutes or until fish is no longer translucent at the thickest part and flakes easily when tested with a fork. (Cooking time will vary depending upon the thickness of the fish.)
7. Garnish with orange slices, if desired.

Catfish Tidbits

Everything You Ever Wanted to Know about Farm-Raised Catfish

Catfish Are Well Brought Up

Commercially raised catfish are top-feeders raised on high-protein food pellets in pollution-free ponds.

Catfish eggs hatch in about a week. The tiny fry grow to 4- to 7-inch fingerlings, which graduate to the food-fish pond, then mature to dinner tables everywhere.

Small Fry to Frying Pan?

Catfish Make Money

Farm-raised catfish is a $4 billion industry in the United States. On the average, Americans eat one pound of catfish per year, but that is expected to double by the year 2010, according to the Catfish Farmers of America.

Catfish Love the South

Catfish farming, or aquaculture, is concentrated in Mississippi, Arkansas, Alabama, and Louisiana.

A new generation of farm-raised catfish has been genetically engineered to grow 20% to 25% faster than most other catfish and to use food more efficiently.

Supercatfish on the Way

Catfish Baked in Mushroom-Wine Sauce

This is a quick and easy dish that tastes great and looks elegant.

Easy
Serves 2

1 tablespoon vegetable oil
1 tablespoon butter or margarine
1 cup fresh mushrooms, sliced
¼ cup green onions, chopped
1 garlic clove, minced
¼ cup white wine
1 tablespoon fresh parsley, chopped
2 catfish fillets, 4 to 6 ounces each
Salt and pepper to taste
Paprika
Cooking spray or vegetable oil
Parsley (optional)
Lemon slices (optional)

1. Preheat oven to 400°. Heat oil and melt butter or margarine together in a heavy skillet. Add mushrooms, onions, and garlic, and sauté until mushrooms become translucent.
2. Add wine and bring to simmer. Remove pan from heat and stir in chopped parsley.
3. Rinse catfish under cool, running water and pat dry with paper towels. Sprinkle with salt, pepper, and paprika on both sides.
4. Place fillets in one layer in a baking dish lightly coated with cooking spray or vegetable oil. Pour mushroom-wine sauce over fillets. Bake for 10 to 20 minutes or until fish is no longer translucent at the thickest part and flakes easily when tested with a fork. (Cooking times will vary depending upon the thickness of the fish.)
5. Garnish with parsley and lemon slices, if desired.

Summer's Garden Catfish

This is a perfect dish for wonderful, ripe tomatoes from either your garden or the local produce stand.

Very Easy
Serves 4

4 catfish fillets, 4 to 6 ounces each
Cooking spray or vegetable oil
¼ cup prepared Italian dressing
Salt and pepper to taste
2 tomatoes, sliced
1 small onion, sliced and separated into rings
2 tablespoons fresh basil, chopped
½ cup grated cheddar cheese

1. Preheat oven to 400°.
2. Rinse catfish under cool, running water and pat dry with paper towels.
3. Lightly coat a baking dish with cooking spray or vegetable oil, and place fillets in it in a single layer .
4. Pour Italian dressing over fillets. Sprinkle with salt and pepper.
5. Arrange tomatoes and onions on top of fish in overlapping pattern. Sprinkle with chopped fresh basil.
6. Bake for 10 to 20 minutes or until fish is no longer translucent at the thickest part and flakes easily when tested with a fork. (Cooking time will vary depending upon the thickness of the fish.)
7. Sprinkle cheese over fish and vegetables and bake 2 to 3 minutes longer or until cheese is melted.

Notes:

6 Soups and Such

Five Soups and a Sandwich

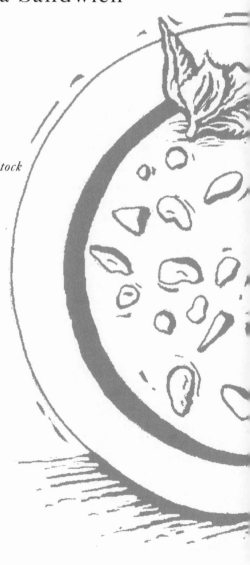

76 *Hints for Making Fish Stock*
78 Carolina Catfish Soup
80 Catfish Corn Chowder
81 Mediterranean Catfish Stew
83 Oriental Noodle Soup
84 Expandable Catfish Stew
85 Spicy Catfish Sandwich

Hints for Making

A good stock is the key to a great soup. Use one pound of fish heads and bones for each quart of water. Shrimp shells are also appropriate for stock. Rinse fish parts under cool, running water before cooking. For each quart of water, add the following ingredients:

Fish or shells
1 to 2 ribs celery, coarsely chopped
1 carrot, coarsely chopped
1 onion, coarsely chopped
2 to 4 sprigs fresh parsley
1 bay leaf
2 to 3 sprigs fresh thyme, if available
Juice of 1 lemon
Lemon slices
¼ teaspoon salt
1 teaspoon peppercorns

Fish Stock

Put fish or shells in water and bring to a boil, then add all remaining ingredients. Turn down heat and simmer for about 20 to 30 minutes uncovered. Strain stock and discard solids. Store liquid in a covered container in the refrigerator or freezer for future use. Freeze stock in ice cube trays, then store cubes in a heavy, sealed plastic bag. You can then remove the exact amount of stock you need without thawing the entire batch. Bring any stored stock to a full boil before using. White wine may also be added to the stock to replace an equal amount of water.

In place of fish, stock can be made from chicken broth or fish, chicken, or vegetable bouillon (if bouillon is used, omit salt). Also, a combination of fish stock and other liquids (broth or bouillon) can be used. A commercially prepared broth or bouillon can be made to taste more like homemade by simmering it for 5 to 10 minutes with chopped onion, carrot, celery, some parsley, and other herbs or seasonings. Clam juice, either full strength or mixed half and half with water, can also be substituted.

Carolina Catfish Soup

This is a very "forgiving" recipe. More potatoes or carrots or fewer slices of onion won't affect the overall recipe. Use what you have. For more guests, double the amounts.

Easy
Serves 4

4 slices of bacon, cut into 1-inch pieces
1 cup onions, chopped
2 to 3 ribs celery, chopped
2 carrots, chopped
3 cups fish, chicken, or vegetable stock (additional stock may be used in step 3)
1 14.5-ounce can diced or chopped tomatoes with juice
2 cups white potatoes, diced
½ teaspoon salt
½ teaspoon pepper
1 pound catfish fillets, cut into 1- to 2-inch cubes
1 teaspoon dried thyme
1 teaspoon dried basil
Hot pepper sauce (optional)

1. Cook bacon in a heavy soup pot over medium heat until slightly browned but not crisp.
2. Sauté onion, celery, and carrots in bacon drippings for 3 to 5 minutes until onion is translucent.
3. Add stock, canned tomatoes with juice, potatoes, salt, and pepper. Simmer covered for 15 to 20 minutes. (If bouillon is used for stock, liquid will be salty. Taste and add salt sparingly or omit it.) For a thinner soup, add more stock at this point.
4. Rinse catfish under cool, running water and pat dry with paper towels. Cut into 1- to 2-inch cubes.

5. Add catfish cubes, thyme, and basil. Cook for 5 minutes or until fish is no longer translucent at the thickest part and flakes easily when tested with a fork.
6. If you like more zip in your soup, add a few dashes of hot pepper sauce.

The Incredible Walking Catfish

One species of catfish has developed air-breathing organs and can migrate across dry land. The "walking catfish" originated in Southeast Asia. In the late 1960s, it was imported into the United States and its progeny were discovered near Boca Raton, Florida. It "walks" by a slithering motion accompanied by a thrashing of the tail. A stout spine in each pectoral fin helps with balance, and a modified gill arch forms an air chamber to help the fish breathe air.

The upside-down catfish, found in the Nile River, relaxes by swimming on its back.

The Topsy-Turvy Catfish

Catfish Corn Chowder

You can modify the spiciness in this zesty corn chowder by substituting plain tomato juice for tangy juice and leaving out the jalapeno pepper.

Easy
Serves 2 to 3

2 tablespoons vegetable oil
1 clove garlic, minced
1 tablespoon jalapeno pepper, seeded and diced (optional)
1 onion, chopped
16-ounce can spicy tomato juice or Bloody Mary mix
8 ounces fish, chicken, or vegetable stock
1½ cups white potato, diced
¼ teaspoon salt
⅛ teaspoon pepper
1 package frozen corn or one 16-ounce can corn, drained
½ teaspoon dried basil
2 catfish fillets, cut into 2-inch cubes

1. Heat oil in a heavy soup pot over medium heat. Sauté garlic, pepper, and onion for 3 to 5 minutes until onion is translucent.
2. Add tomato juice and stock. Stir well.
3. Add potato, salt, and pepper and simmer covered for 15 minutes. (If bouillon is used for stock, liquid will be salty. Taste chowder and add salt sparingly or omit it.)
4. Add corn and basil. Simmer covered until corn is heated.
5. Rinse catfish under cool, running water and pat dry with paper towels. Cut into 2-inch cubes.
6. Add catfish and cook for 5 minutes or until fish is no longer translucent at the thickest part and flakes easily when tested with a fork.

Mediterranean Catfish Stew

Red wine and oregano give this easy soup a taste of the sunny Mediterranean.

Moderately Easy
Serves 6 to 8

2 to 3 tablespoons olive oil
1 cup onion, chopped
2 cloves garlic, minced
1 cup celery, chopped
1 cup red, yellow, or green bell pepper, chopped
2 14.5-ounce cans diced tomatoes with juice
1 bay leaf
½ teaspoon cumin
1 teaspoon oregano
Salt and pepper to taste
½ cup red wine
3 cups fish, chicken, or vegetable stock
1 pound catfish, cut into 2-inch cubes
Cayenne pepper to taste
Assorted shellfish, cleaned (optional)
3 to 4 cups cooked white rice (optional)

1. Heat oil in a heavy soup pot over medium heat. Sauté onion, garlic, celery, and pepper 3 to 5 minutes until onion is translucent.
2. Add tomatoes with juice, bay leaf, spices, red wine, and stock. (If bouillon is used for stock, the liquid will be salty. Taste and add salt sparingly or omit it.)
3. Simmer covered for half an hour.
4. Rinse catfish under cool, running water and pat dry with paper towels. Lightly sprinkle fillets with cayenne pepper. Cut fish into 2-inch cubes.
5. Add catfish cubes to stew and simmer 5 minutes or until fish is

no longer translucent at the thickest part and flakes easily when tested with a fork.

6. If you like a thicker, more gumbolike soup, you may add shellfish about 2 minutes after adding catfish to the soup. Cook until done.

7. If desired, add ½ cup cooked rice to each serving bowl before ladling in the soup. Be sure to remove the bay leaf!

The Man-Eating Catfish

The huge sheatfish, or wels catfish, of Europe, which supposedly can weigh as much as 650 pounds and can grow to 13 feet in length, has been accused of attacking animals and small children.

The electric catfish of Africa can generate a shock of 350 volts. Shock treatment for epilepsy was once administered by this catfish.

The Shocking Electric Catfish

The Watch-My-Fins Catfish

The dorsal and pectoral fins of this fish are sometimes edged in sharp, poisonous spines that can inflict painful wounds.

Oriental Noodle Soup

The world's easiest soup recipe is also quick and tasty.

Very Easy
Serves 2

3 cups water
½ pound catfish fillets, cut into 1-inch cubes
3-ounce package oriental soup mix
Juice of 1 lemon or lime

1. Bring water to boil in a medium saucepan.
2. Rinse catfish under cool, running water and pat dry with paper towels. Cut into 1-inch cubes. Add catfish and simmer 5 minutes.
3. Add noodles from soup mix. Cook according to package directions, approximately 2 to 3 minutes.
4. Check catfish for doneness. It should no longer be translucent at the thickest part and should flake easily when tested with a fork.
5. Add seasoning packet from soup mix and stir in lemon or lime juice.

The glass catfish is almost transparent and is frequently seen in aquariums.

The See-Through Catfish

Expandable Catfish Stew

This easy recipe is a family favorite from Donna Pass. The great thing is that this recipe easily expands according to the number of folks you expect to drop by for dinner.

Very Easy
Serves as many as you want

For each person:
1 catfish fillet, 4 to 6 ounces
1 medium or large onion, sliced
1 medium or large potato, sliced (approximately
⅜ inches thick)
Salt and pepper to taste
Margarine to taste (or dried, granulated butter
for a reduced fat version)

1. Rinse catfish under cool, running water and pat dry with paper towels.
2. Arrange onions, potatoes, and fillets in alternating layers (beginning with onions) in a covered pan or Dutch oven. Sprinkle each layer with salt and pepper. Cooking pot should be large enough to hold all the ingredients with a few inches to spare at the top.
3. Margarine or dried butter granules can be added to each layer with salt and pepper or sprinkled onto the top of the layer only.
4. Add approximately 1 to 2 inches of water. Bring to a boil; then lower heat to a simmer and cover. Cook 20 to 30 minutes or until vegetables are tender and fish is no longer translucent at the thickest part and flakes easily when tested with a fork.

Spicy Catfish Sandwich

A spectacular sauce is the perfect complement for the light, sweet taste of the pan-fried catfish.

Easy
Serves 2 to 4

Sauce:
½ cup mayonnaise or salad dressing (regular or low fat)
1 teaspoon Worcestershire sauce
1 teaspoon garlic powder
1 teaspoon cayenne pepper
2 tablespoons onion, minced
2 tablespoons pickle, chopped (sweet, sour, or dill)
¼ teaspoon hot pepper sauce
¼ teaspoon salt

1 to 2 tablespoons vegetable oil
1 to 2 tablespoons butter or margarine
4 catfish fillets, 4 to 6 ounces each
Juice of fresh lemon
4 buns of choice

1. Mix all sauce ingredients. Taste. Add more spices to your taste. Mix again. Refrigerate and allow flavors to blend for about an hour.
2. Rinse catfish under cool, running water and pat dry with paper towels. Cut fillets to bun size. Drizzle the juice of one lemon over the fish.
3. Heat oil and melt butter in a heavy skillet over medium heat. The oil should cover the bottom of the skillet to a depth of ⅛ to ¼ inch. Heat until oil and butter bubble.
4. Add catfish and sauté for 2 to 4 minutes on each side until fish is golden brown, is no longer translucent at the thickest part, and flakes easily when tested with a fork.
5. Place cooked catfish on buns. Top with generous helpings of spicy sauce.

Notes:

7 Catfish Condiments

Remoulade and Other Saucy Accents

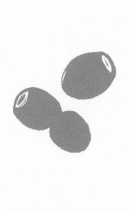

Hints for Storing Herbs and Spices 88

Easy Remoulade Sauce 90

Quick Tartar Sauce 91

Cilantro Tartar Sauce 92

Spicy Red Sauce 93

Low-Fat Horseradish Sauce 93

Basic Barbecue Sauce 94

Honey-Mustard Dip 95

Hooked on Catfish—Anglers Lure the Elusive Prey 96

Tzatsiki Sauce 97

Low-Fat Yogurt-Mint Sauce 98

Low-Fat Yogurt-Dill Sauce 98

Summer Salsa 99

Fried Catfish Dip 100

Hints for Storing

Store spices tightly covered in a cool, dark place. Don't keep spices or dried herbs longer than six months.

To reconstitute the flavor of dried herbs, soak them in lemon juice, wine, oil, or another liquid to be added to the dish you're preparing.

Store fresh herbs in the refrigerator by putting the stems of the "bouquet" of herbs into a jar or glass filled with water. Cover the herbs with a plastic bag or plastic wrap and secure with a rubber band around the container.

You can freeze fresh herbs. Some, such as rosemary and thyme, do best frozen on the stem after being rinsed in cold water. For others, such as mint and sage, snip the leaves and place in a freezer bag. Store them in a spot in the freezer where they won't be crushed.

Another easy way to store your herbs is in a freezer ice tray. Place the snipped herbs in a tray compartment, fill with water or stock, and freeze, covering the trays tightly with plastic wrap. When frozen, store the ice cubes in a freezer-safe storage container or bag. When you want to add herbs to a stew, soup, or gumbo, drop in the herbed cubes. You can also use butter as a storage medium. Soften butter, add minced herbs, form into patties, and freeze in a freezer-safe container. Thaw when needed and use in cooking.

Herbs & Spices

You can store ginger in the refrigerator for up to two weeks by wrapping it tightly in plastic wrap. Or you can peel ginger root, cut it into pieces, and place it in a jar filled with white wine or sherry. Cover the jar tightly and refrigerate. Ginger can also be frozen. Peel and mince or cut ginger into sections, put into plastic bags, and freeze. Store "red spices," such as cayenne pepper, chili powder, paprika, and curry, in tightly sealed containers in the refrigerator.

Easy Remoulade Sauce

This easy sauce is wonderful with catfish and also goes well with raw or steamed vegetables.

Moderately Easy
Makes 1+ cup

1 cup mayonnaise or salad dressing (regular or low fat)
1 tablespoon onion, minced
1 tablespoon celery, diced
1 tablespoon cider vinegar
1 tablespoon prepared horseradish
1½ tablespoons Dijon or Creole mustard
1 teaspoon paprika
½ teaspoon salt
Dash of hot pepper sauce
½ teaspoon Worcestershire sauce
1 teaspoon sugar
1 clove garlic, minced

1. Combine all ingredients in a bowl.
2. Taste and add more seasonings or mayonnaise to suit your taste.
3. Mix again and refrigerate in a covered container.

OLD CHINESE PROVERB:
Give a boy a fish to eat, and he
will be happy for one day.
    Teach a boy to fish, and he
will be happy for the rest of
his life.

MODERN VERSION:
Teach a boy to fish, and he'll sit
in a boat all day and drink beer.

Quick Tartar Sauce

This tartar sauce is easy to make at home.

Very Easy
Makes 1 cup

1 cup of mayonnaise or salad dressing (regular or low fat)
2 tablespoons sweet pickle mix, drained
1 tablespoon onion, minced

1. Combine ingredients.
2. Taste and add more seasonings or mayonnaise to your taste.
3. Mix again and refrigerate in a covered container.

Cilantro Tartar Sauce

If you like to experiment, substitute Greek kalamata olives for ripe olives. This is wonderful on a fried catfish sandwich. Add a chopped, hard-boiled egg to any left-over sauce to make an easy egg salad.

Easy
Makes 1+ cup

1 cup mayonnaise (regular or low fat)
1 tablespoon Dijon mustard
3 tablespoons ripe black olives, pitted and chopped
2 tablespoons capers, drained
1 teaspoon dried cilantro or 1 tablespoon fresh cilantro, chopped

1. Combine all ingredients except cilantro.
2. Taste and adjust seasonings. Add cilantro incrementally, ½ teaspoon at a time, to your taste. Taste and adjust again, adding more mayonnaise, mustard, capers, or olives to suit your taste.
3. Mix again and refrigerate in a covered container.

Spicy Red Sauce

This is another easy condiment that's a must with fish of any kind.

Very Easy
Makes 1+ cup

1 cup catsup
1 tablespoon lemon juice
1 teaspoon prepared horseradish
Dash of hot pepper sauce
1 teaspoon Worcestershire sauce

1. Combine ingredients.
2. Taste and add more seasonings or catsup to suit your taste.
3. Mix again and refrigerate in a covered container.

Low-Fat Horseradish Sauce

This works well with poached or grilled catfish to give that extra zing.

Very Easy
Makes 1 cup

4 tablespoons plain, fat-free yogurt
4 tablespoons low-fat mayonnaise
2 tablespoons prepared horseradish
1 tablespoon onion, minced
¼ teaspoon paprika

1. Combine ingredients.
2. Taste and add more seasoning, yogurt, or mayonnaise to suit your taste.
3. Mix again and refrigerate in a covered container.

Basic Barbecue Sauce

Every region of the country has its own barbecue preferences. Carolina Tarheels prefer a vinegar base, while Georgians like tomato. This recipe can be doctored up or down to please any taste buds. Use your favorite on grilled catfish fillets.

Very Easy
Makes ½ cup

2 tablespoons butter or margarine
2 tablespoons catsup
2 tablespoons vinegar
2 tablespoons Worcestershire sauce
1 teaspoon to 1 tablespoon brown sugar

1. Melt butter or margarine in a small sauce pan. Do not let it brown.
2. Add the catsup, vinegar, and Worcestershire. Add brown sugar incrementally, beginning with 1 teaspoon, to suit your taste. Mix well and heat. The base will be tart and vinegary. Adjust ingredients to suit your taste.
3. Use at once or refrigerate in a covered container.

Honey-Mustard Dip

Use this as a dipping sauce with fried catfish fingers.

Easy
Makes ½ cup

¼ cup honey
1½ tablespoons Dijon mustard
2 to 3 tablespoons lemon juice

1. Combine ingredients.
2. Taste and add more of any ingredient to suit your taste.
3. Mix again. Refrigerate in a covered container. Remove from refrigerator about half an hour before serving.

Hooked on Catfish

Anglers Lure the Elusive Prey

A long-time fisherman from south Georgia advises using worms, crickets, and "cut bait" (any kind of cut-up fish) to catch catfish. This fisherman says most cats will bite any kind of bait, and he likes a good, ol', down-home cane pole. A veteran fisherman from Minnesota echoes the effectiveness of a bamboo cane pole and fishing line when fishing for cats, just like Huck Finn and Tom Sawyer used.

A young catfish expert from Tennessee says that yellow cats (flatheads), found in rivers, like live bait. Channel cats (willow cats), which live in ponds, will bite any kind of bait, such as worms, minnows, crickets, grasshoppers, liver, and "stinking bait." He prefers a good rod and reel with a 20- to 40-pound line.

Cat fishermen going for records use an array of high-tech fishing gear, with rods made especially for catfish. For reels, they look for a solid frame and gears tough enough to handle the "big blues" (*Ictalurus furcatus*). Here are some big-blue rod-and-reel records, which are probably being broken as you read this: (On trotlines, the record big blues top 125 pounds.)

111 pounds (Alabama)	85.9 pounds (California)
103 pounds (Missouri)	82.5 pounds (Tennessee)
100.5 pounds (Nebraska)	82 pounds (Kansas)
97 pounds (South Dakota)	79.1 pounds (Illinois)
96 pounds (Arkansas)	78.5 pounds (North Carolina)
96 pounds (Texas/Oklahoma border)	75 pounds (Indiana)
93 pounds (Mississippi)	61.5 pounds (Florida)

Tzatsiki Sauce

There are many derivatives of this sauce. Our thanks to Kathryn Coumanis of Mobile, Alabama, for the basics of this one. It's delicious with Athenian Broiled Catfish.

Moderately Easy
Makes 1+ cup

1 cup plain yogurt, drained (regular or low fat)
1 cucumber, peeled and seeded
½ teaspoon salt
1 clove garlic, minced
1 tablespoon olive oil
1 or 2 squeezes of lemon juice

1. Drain yogurt through a clean cheesecloth or colander to remove liquid.
2. While yogurt is draining, peel cucumber, remove seeds, and slice lengthwise.
3. Grate cucumber slices, sprinkle with salt, and drain through cheesecloth or a colander for about an hour. Squeeze cucumbers gently with a clean cloth or paper towels to remove bitter liquid.
4. Combine cucumber and garlic with yogurt and olive oil. Mix well.
5. Add a squeeze of lemon juice. Mix again. Taste and adjust with more garlic or lemon.
6. Mix again and refrigerate in a covered container. Flavors need to mingle for at least an hour before serving.

Low-Fat Yogurt-Mint Sauce

These two yogurt recipes are low fat, fresh tasting, and easy to prepare.

Very Easy
Makes 1 cup

1 cup plain, fat-free yogurt
1 tablespoon fresh mint, chopped
1 to 2 squeezes lemon juice

1. Drain yogurt through clean cheesecloth or colander to remove liquid.
2. Add chopped fresh mint and a squeeze of lemon juice. Mix well.
3. Taste and adjust mint and lemon juice. Mix again and refrigerate in a covered container.

Low-Fat Yogurt-Dill Sauce

Very easy
Makes 1+ cup

1 cup plain, fat-free yogurt
1 medium cucumber, peeled and seeded
3 tablespoons low-fat mayonnaise
2 tablespoons fresh dill, chopped
1 large clove garlic, minced
Salt to taste

1. Drain yogurt through clean cheesecloth or colander to remove liquid.
2. Grate cucumber and combine all ingredients.
3. Taste and adjust dill and garlic. Mix again and refrigerate in a covered container.

Summer Salsa

Plum tomatoes are preferred, but any ripe tomato will work. It's up to you to adjust the spiciness. This is excellent as a garnish with grilled catfish.

Easy
Makes 1+ cup

1 cup tomatoes, peeled and diced
¼ cup green or red onion, diced
1 tablespoon jalapeno pepper, minced
1 tablespoon vegetable oil
1 tablespoon fresh lime juice
Salt and pepper to taste
2 cloves garlic, minced
1 teaspoon dried cilantro or 1 tablespoon fresh cilantro, chopped
¼ teaspoon dried oregano
2 dashes of hot pepper sauce
1 tablespoon fresh parsley, chopped (optional)

1. Combine tomatoes, onions, and pepper.
2. In a separate bowl, whisk together oil, lime juice, spices, herbs, and pepper sauce. Taste and adjust seasonings. Add mixture to vegetable mix.
3. Refrigerate in a covered container for several hours. Stir, taste, and adjust spices. Remember: it's easier to add jalapenos and hot sauce than to remove them!

Fried Catfish Dip

Thanks to Valrie Spence of Dawson, Georgia, for sharing her ideas on this wonderful dip.

Very Easy
2+ cups

1 pint mayonnaise (regular or low fat)
1 tablespoon chives, minced
1 tablespoon parsley, minced
1 tablespoon prepared horseradish
1 tablespoon mustard
1 large onion, diced

1. Combine all ingredients.
2. Taste and add more seasonings or mayonnaise to suit your taste.
3. Mix again and refrigerate.

8 Catfish Companions

Coleslaw and Hoppin' John, to Name a Few

102   *Pond Draining—A Time for Feasting*
103   Quick Coleslaw
104   Moravian Coleslaw
105   Lynda's Easy Potato Salad
106   Old-Fashioned Potato Salad
107   Tangy Potato Salad
108   Anything-Goes Marinated Salad
110   Black-Eyed Pea Salad
111   Hoppin' John
112   Sweet Southern Dills

Pond Draining

A Time for Feasting

If you're lucky enough to have friends or relatives who still live on a farm, get yourself invited to a pond draining, or pond seining. A hot summer's day will find usually dignified men dressed in overalls and whoopin' and hollerin' and splashing around in the shallow, muddy water, trying to catch fish in seining nets or with their bare hands. It's a time for draining and for feasting as well.

A pond draining is held every few years to clear out the large fish and to restore balance to an overpopulated pond. The responsibilities at a pond draining are pretty much divided along gender lines—the men and boys catch the fish by any means imaginable, and the women and girls gut and fry the fish. But times are changing, and occasionally you do see a switch in roles.

Before the day is out, you'll have the chance to bite into succulent fried catfish and other pond-dwellers, as well as sample a colorful variety of catfish companions. These side dishes almost always include coleslaw and recipes made from anything else that's in season in the garden. Recipes for the requisite hushpuppies; desserts; and a few nontraditional dishes, such as black-eyed pea salad, can be found in this cookbook.

Now pour yourself a tall glass of sweet iced tea and have a good time!

Quick Coleslaw

Depending on your leanings toward mayonnaise or vinegar dressing, the recipe can be easily adjusted.

Easy
Serves 4 to 6

4 cups green cabbage, chopped or shredded
3 green onions, chopped
1 medium carrot, shredded or grated
½ cup mayonnaise
2 tablespoons vinegar (cider or red wine)
1 teaspoon sugar
Salt and pepper to taste
1 teaspoon celery seed (optional)

1. Mix cabbage, onions, and carrot in a large bowl. Toss lightly.
2. Combine mayonnaise, vinegar, and sugar. Taste and adjust seasonings. Add salt, pepper, and celery seed, if desired.
3. Pour dressing over slaw, and toss lightly. Cover and refrigerate so the flavors blend.

Moravian Coleslaw

The Moravians were a Protestant sect who fled Europe because of religious persecution. They first settled in Pennsylvania and later in Salem, North Carolina. This easy recipe carries a hint of the old world.

Easy
Serves 4 to 6

1 cup white wine vinegar
1 cup water
1 cup sugar
2 tablespoons vegetable oil
1 head cabbage, sliced or grated
1 onion, thinly sliced
1 bell pepper, minced
1 carrot, grated
1 teaspoon salt
½ teaspoon pepper
1 teaspoon celery seed (optional)

1. Bring the vinegar, water, sugar and oil to a boil. Simmer and let cook for 2 to 3 minutes. Allow to cool.
2. Combine other ingredients in a large bowl. Pour cool dressing over the mix. Refrigerate for 24 hours.

Lynda's Easy Potato Salad

Lynda Tatum of Atlanta has been whipping up this dish for her family for years.

Easy
Serves 6

3 pounds red-skinned potatoes, unpeeled
1 teaspoon salt
2 to 3 ribs celery, chopped
3 to 4 green onions, chopped

Dressing:
1 cup mayonnaise
1 tablespoon white vinegar
1 tablespoon mustard
Salt and pepper to taste

1. Scrub potatoes and prick skins with the tines of a fork.
2. Cook potatoes in boiling water; add 1 teaspoon salt to the boiling water during cooking. Test potatoes for doneness with a fork; they should be tender.
3. Quarter each potato, leaving skins on. Add chopped celery and onions to potatoes. Toss lightly.
4. To make dressing, add vinegar, mustard, salt, and pepper to mayonnaise. Pour dressing over salad and toss lightly. Cover and refrigerate so the flavors blend.

Old-Fashioned Potato Salad

This is the potato salad served throughout the South at church picnics and family reunions.

Moderately Easy
Serves 4 to 6

4 large (or 10 to 15 small) potatoes
2 to 3 ribs celery, chopped
3 to 4 green onions, chopped
½ cup sweet pickle relish (or chopped sweet pickle)
2 hard-boiled eggs, chopped

Dressing:
1 cup mayonnaise
1 tablespoon cider vinegar
1 teaspoon sugar
½ teaspoon dried mustard
1 teaspoon salt
1 teaspoon pepper

1. Scrub potatoes and prick skins once or twice with the tines of a fork.
2. Boil potatoes until tender. Check doneness with a fork.
3. Allow to cool. Peel and cube potatoes. (You should have approximately 4 cups of potatoes.) Add celery, onions, pickle relish, and chopped eggs. Toss lightly.
4. To make dressing, add vinegar, sugar, mustard, salt, and pepper to mayonnaise. Taste and adjust seasonings.
5. Pour dressing over salad and toss lightly. Cover and refrigerate so flavors blend.

Tangy Potato Salad

This is potato salad with an attitude!

Easy
Serves 4

1½ pounds red-skinned potatoes
1 teaspoon salt
2 tablespoons olive oil
1 clove garlic, minced
¼ cup fresh parsley, chopped
1 tablespoon lemon rind, grated
2 tablespoons lemon juice
Lemon slices (optional)
Sprigs of parsley (optional)

1. Scrub potatoes and prick skins with the tines of a fork.
2. Boil in salted water until tender but firm. Drain potatoes and allow to cool.
3. Cut potatoes into halves or quarters, depending on size of potatoes.
4. Heat oil in a heavy skillet and add garlic. Do not allow garlic to turn brown. Turn off heat. Add potatoes, parsley, grated lemon rind, and lemon juice. Toss lightly. May be served at room temperature or chilled.
5. Garnish with lemon slices and sprigs of parsley, if desired.

Anything-Goes Marinated Salad

Val McIntyre shared a recipe years ago that is the inspiration for this salad. You can choose vegetables according to what's in season or to your own personal preference. It's important to blanche the broccoli and cauliflower before putting this recipe together. Note that this recipe requires 8 to 24 hours of marinating in the refrigerator, so make it about a day before you need it.

Moderately Easy
Serves 6 to 8

1 head broccoli
1 head cauliflower
1 bowl ice water
1 to 2 medium zucchini, sliced
1 to 2 medium yellow squashes, sliced
1 large red, yellow, or Vidalia onion, chopped,
or 5 to 7 green onions, sliced
10 to 12 radishes, sliced
8 ounces commercially prepared oil and vinegar,
Greek, or Italian salad dressing
salt and pepper to taste
1 to 2 ripe tomatoes, chopped (optional)
Fresh parsley or basil, chopped (optional)

1. Chop broccoli and cauliflower into bite-size pieces. Bring a large pot of water to a boil. Prepare a bowl of ice and water.
2. Blanche broccoli and cauliflower in boiling water for 1 to 2 minutes. Put immediately into icy water. Drain well.
3. Mix all vegetables in a large bowl. Pour 6 to 8 ounces of prepared dressing over the vegetables. Any oil-and-vinegar-based, non-creamy dressing will do.
4. Cover vegetables tightly and refrigerate for 8 to 24 hours. Invert container several times so all vegetables are covered by the dressing.
5. Taste before serving. Add salt and pepper to taste. Add ripe tomatoes and fresh parsley or basil as garnish, if desired.

Black-Eyed Pea Salad

This is another easy, prepare-ahead, take-along salad that offers many opportunities for experimentation. The wild rice gives the dish a wonderful nutty taste.

> *Moderately Easy*
> *Serves 4 to 6*

> 2 cups cooked black-eyed peas (canned or frozen peas may be used)
> 2 cups cooked rice (wild rice may be substituted)
> ½ cup red, yellow, or green onion, minced
> ¼ cup radishes, chopped
> ½ cup green bell pepper, chopped
> ½ cup celery, chopped
> 1 tablespoon jalapeno pepper, minced (optional)

> *Dressing:*
> ¼ cup vegetable oil
> ¼ cup red wine vinegar
> ¼ teaspoon garlic powder
> ½ teaspoon dried oregano
> Salt and pepper to taste
> ¼ cup fresh parsley, minced (optional)

1. Mix first 7 ingredients together. Toss lightly.
2. To make dressing, whisk together oil, vinegar, garlic powder, oregano, salt, and pepper. Add parsley, if desired, and whisk again. Taste and adjust seasonings.
3. Pour dressing over salad. Toss lightly. Cover and refrigerate so flavors blend.

Hoppin' John

This is a must in the South on New Year's Day, served along with pork and greens, but it's also good with fried or grilled catfish. Fresh black-eyed peas are terrific if you can get them, but you can cheat and use canned or frozen peas. Serve this dish hot with cornbread.

Easy
Serves 4 to 6

1 pound dried black-eyed peas
¼ pound salt pork or ham hocks
3 cups cooked white rice
Salt and pepper to taste
Hot pepper sauce (optional)

1. Sort through peas and remove any broken peas or other debris. Rinse peas thoroughly and soak overnight in a covered pot.
2. Drain peas. Add fresh water to cover. Add salt pork or ham hocks.
3. Bring to a boil, then reduce heat and cover tightly. Simmer for 1 to 1½ hours or until peas are firm but not mushy. Only a small amount of water should remain in the pot.
4. Add cooked rice to pot and mix gently. Check for taste. Add salt and pepper.
5. Serve with hot pepper sauce on the side, if desired.

Sweet Southern Dills

We first tasted these great pickles in Georgia but since then have discovered similar recipes from all around the South. Tart and sweet at the same time, they are a must with fried catfish. Note that the pickles need to marinate for 24 hours, so this is a make-ahead recipe.

Easy
Makes 1 quart

1 quart jar dill pickles, whole or sliced
½ cup water
½ cup white vinegar
1½ to 1⅔ cups sugar
1 teaspoon celery or mustard seed

1. Rinse pickles in cold water. Pat dry with paper towels. Slice into strips or chunks.
2. Simmer water, vinegar, sugar, and celery or mustard seed in a pot for 2 to 3 minutes. Take off heat. Let liquid cool. (Taste vinegar/sugar mix. If too tart, add more sugar and reheat until sugar melts.)
3. Replace pickles in their original jar and cover with cooled liquid. Refrigerate and allow pickles to marinate for at least 24 hours. Invert jar several times during the marinating period so all pickles are covered by liquid.

9 Foreign Friends

Great Side Dishes from Around the World

Availability of Ingredients   114
South-of-the-Border Salad   115
Greek Salad   116
LaDonna's Cheese Strata   117
Tuscan Bread Salad   118
Tabouli   119
Oriental Cucumber Salad   120
Oriental Coleslaw   121
Italian Tomato Salad   122

Availability of Ingredients

We promised in the introduction that the ingredients in our recipes would be readily accessible. All ingredients, even those that sound exotic, are available in the ethnic or produce sections of major supermarket chains, even in small towns. Look for jalapeno peppers (fresh, canned, or jarred), fresh ginger root, rice wine vinegar, hoisin sauce, balsamic

vinegar, sesame oil, sesame seeds, and feta cheese. Many supermarket produce sections, farmers' markets, and garden shops also sell pots of fresh parsley, basil, oregano, thyme, dill, marjoram, cilantro, tarragon, and other culinary herbs for your windowsill or garden.

If an ingredient isn't immediately available in your area, we encourage experimentation and substitution: oregano for

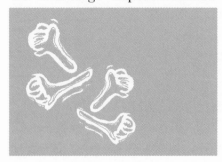

marjoram, white cider vinegar for rice vinegar, and red pepper flakes for a fresh serrano pepper. The more you experiment, the more you make a recipe your own specialty.

South-of-the-Border Salad

This colorful salad from Latanja McKay of Boynton Beach, Florida, is a real crowd-pleaser.

Easy
Serves 6

½ 15-ounce can black beans, rinsed and drained
½ 15-ounce can red beans, rinsed and drained
1 10-ounce package frozen corn, thawed
4 plum tomatoes, seeded and diced
1 jalapeno pepper, seeded and minced
½ red onion, minced
⅓ cup fresh cilantro, chopped
2 tablespoons lime juice
1 tablespoon olive oil
1 teaspoon ground cumin
¼ teaspoon salt
¼ teaspoon pepper

1. Combine first 7 ingredients in a bowl.
2. Whisk together the remaining ingredients. Pour over bean-and-corn mixture.
3. Toss lightly. May be served immediately or chilled.

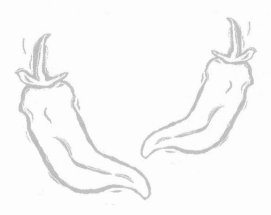

Greek Salad

There are many versions of Greek salad, but this one, served in a small restaurant overlooking the Aegean on the island of Rhodes, is memorable. Other recipes call for bell peppers, radishes, and/or celery, so experiment. Grilled catfish is a perfect companion.

Moderately Easy
Serves 4

4 cups salad greens, torn
2 tomatoes, cut into ⅛ sections
1 onion, sliced into rounds, or 3 to 4 green onions, sliced
1 cucumber, peeled and sliced
12 pitted black olives, whole or sliced
8 pepperoncini (salad peppers)
½ to 1 cup feta cheese, crumbled

Dressing:
¾ cup olive oil
¼ cup red wine vinegar
1 tablespoon lemon juice
1 clove garlic, minced
½ teaspoon dried oregano or ½ tablespoon fresh
Salt and pepper to taste

1. Wash and dry salad greens. Tear into bite-size pieces and place in a large bowl.
2. Add tomatoes, onions, and cucumbers.
3. To make dressing, whisk ingredients together or shake in a tightly closed jar. You may also use commercially prepared Greek salad dressing.
4. Pour over salad and lightly toss. Garnish with black olives, pepperoncini, and feta cheese.

LaDonna's Cheese Strata

This is an easy way to make a soufflé, courtesy of our friend Donna Ball of north Georgia. You can always substitute or add other vegetables and/or cooked ham, turkey, or chicken to your layers. Note that the casserole must be refrigerated before it's cooked, so do allow extra time for that.

Easy
Serves 4

Butter, margarine, or cooking oil or spray
1 medium zucchini, sliced
Fresh or dried basil, oregano, dill, or thyme
Salt and pepper to taste
5 to 6 slices day-old bread, buttered
1 cup cheddar cheese, grated
2 ripe tomatoes, sliced
2 to 3 eggs, beaten
1 to 1½ cups milk

1. Preheat oven to 350°. Lightly coat a 1½-quart casserole dish with butter, margarine, or cooking oil or spray. Be sure to coat the sides well.
2. Cover bottom of casserole with overlapping zucchini slices. Sprinkle with herbs, salt, and pepper.
3. Tear or slice buttered bread into 1-inch cubes. In a bowl, toss bread and cheese until ingredients are well mixed. Place a portion of cheese/bread mixture on top of zucchini.
4. Add a layer of overlapping tomato slices and sprinkle with herbs, salt, and pepper. Cover with another layer of bread and cheese.
5. In a bowl, whisk eggs, milk, salt, and pepper. Pour this mixture over the bread mix. Be sure the bread mix is covered by the liquid.
6. Refrigerate casserole for several hours before cooking, up to 8 hours.
7. Bake for 50 to 60 minutes or until a knife inserted into the center comes out clean.

Tuscan Bread Salad

This is another recipe from Donna Ball, prepared with vine-ripened tomatoes from her garden. She says fresh basil is the key to this recipe and insists you use plenty of dressing.

Very Easy
Serves 4

Loaf of day-old Italian bread, cubed (about 4 cups)
8 to 10 ripe plum tomatoes, cut into rough chunks
1 cup red onion, sliced
1 cup fresh basil leaves
1 clove garlic, minced
1½ teaspoons salt
½ teaspoon black pepper, freshly ground
¼ teaspoon sugar

Dressing:
¾ cup olive oil
⅓ cup red wine vinegar
1 clove garlic, minced
HERBS: oregano, thyme, parsley
(whatever is fresh and available)
Parmesan cheese, freshly grated (optional)

1. Mix bread, tomatoes, onions, basil, garlic, salt, pepper, and sugar. Toss lightly.
2. To make dressing, mix olive oil, vinegar, garlic, and herbs. You may also use a commercially prepared red wine vinegar dressing with an olive-oil base.
3. Pour ¾ cup to 1 cup dressing over the salad. Let salad stand for 20 minutes so flavors can mingle.
4. Serve topped with freshly grated Parmesan cheese, if desired.

Tabouli

This is an extremely versatile dish that cries out for substitutions and originality. It's wonderful to take on a picnic or to a barbecue, and it's great with grilled catfish.

Moderately Easy
Serves 4

1 cup dry bulgur wheat (cracked wheat)
2 cups boiling water
1½ teaspoons salt
⅓ cup fresh lemon juice or lime juice
1½ teaspoons garlic, minced
⅓ cup olive oil
¼ cup fresh mint, chopped
1 cup fresh parsley, chopped
½ cup green onions, chopped
Black pepper, freshly ground
2 medium tomatoes, diced
Optional: chopped green pepper, grated carrot, chopped cooked chickpeas, chopped cucumber, and chopped summer squash

1. Add boiling water and salt to bowl of bulgur. Let stand 20 to 30 minutes. If bulgur is still too firm or chewy, add ¼ cup more boiling water, cover, and let sit 10 more minutes. Drain excess water.
2. Add lemon or lime juice, garlic, oil, mint, parsley, onions, and pepper and mix well. Refrigerate for 2 to 3 hours.
3. Add tomatoes and optional ingredients, as desired. Stir gently. Taste and adjust seasonings.

Oriental Cucumber Salad

This is good as a side dish for Sesame- or Tempura-Fried Catfish or as a dressing for a leafy green salad.

Very Easy
Serves 4 to 6

1 to 2 medium cucumbers, thinly sliced (enough for 2 cups)
⅓ cup white cider vinegar or rice wine vinegar
4 to 6 thin slices fresh ginger root, peeled
2 to 4 teaspoons sugar or to taste
1 teaspoon salt
¼ teaspoon white pepper
Sesame seeds, toasted (optional)*

1. Place cucumbers in small, nonmetallic container.
2. In a separate bowl, mix vinegar, ginger root, sugar, salt, and pepper.
3. Pour over cucumbers and cover container tightly. Refrigerate 2 to 3 hours. Invert container several times during the marinating period so vinegar covers all cucumbers. Drain and serve as a relish or side dish or use with liquid as a salad dressing. Add sesame seeds as a garnish, if desired.

*To toast raw sesame seeds, spread seeds evenly over a baking sheet and bake in a 350° oven for 5 minutes, stirring occasionally. Watch the seeds carefully to avoid burning.

Oriental Coleslaw

The textures in this easy, unusual coleslaw make it a delightful side dish.

Easy
Serves 6 to 8

2 packages oriental noodle soup mix
1 head cabbage, shredded
6 to 8 green onions, thinly sliced
¼ cup almonds, toasted*
¼ cup sesame seeds, toasted*

Dressing:
⅓ cup vegetable oil
2 tablespoons dark sesame oil
⅓ cup rice vinegar
2 tablespoons sugar
1 teaspoon salt
1 teaspoon pepper

1. Discard seasoning packet of oriental soup mix. Cook noodles according to package directions.
2. Combine noodles, shredded cabbage, green onions, almonds, and sesame seeds in a serving bowl.
3. To make dressing, in a small bowl, whisk together oils, vinegar, sugar, salt, and pepper. Add just enough of the dressing to the noodles and cabbage to moisten. Toss lightly and serve.

*To toast raw sesame seeds, spread seeds evenly over a baking sheet and bake in a 350° oven for 5 minutes, stirring occasionally. Toast almonds in the same manner for 5–10 minutes. Watch the nuts carefully to avoid burning.

Italian Tomato Salad

Think warm, sunny afternoons in the Tuscan hills above Florence when you prepare this dish. No salad could be easier or more perfect with fried or grilled catfish.

> *Very Easy*
> *Serves as many as you want*

> Ripe tomatoes
> Mozzarella cheese, sliced
> Salt and pepper to taste
> Basil leaves, whole or cut into thin strips
> Pure, virgin olive oil
> Balsamic vinegar (optional)

1. Slice tomatoes. Arrange on a plate.
2. Slice cheese about ¼ inch thick. Place on top of tomatoes.
3. Top cheese and tomatoes with basil to taste.
4. Sprinkle with salt and pepper.
5. Drizzle with olive oil and vinegar, if desired.

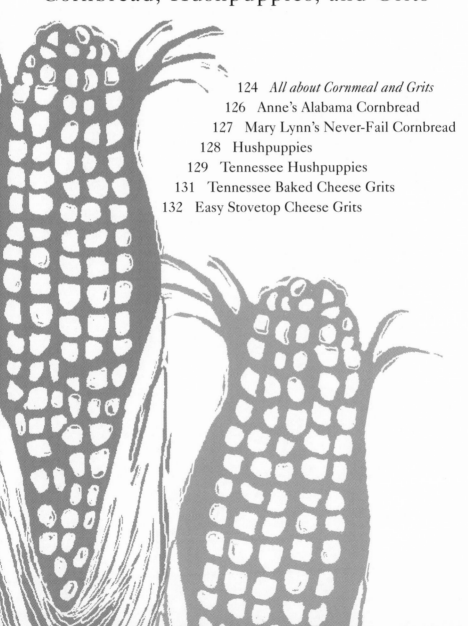

10 Amazing Maize

Cornbread, Hushpuppies, and Grits

124   *All about Cornmeal and Grits*
126   Anne's Alabama Cornbread
127   Mary Lynn's Never-Fail Cornbread
128   Hushpuppies
129   Tennessee Hushpuppies
131   Tennessee Baked Cheese Grits
132   Easy Stovetop Cheese Grits

All about Cornmeal

Early New World explorers seeking gold and fabled cities made a remarkable discovery—corn, truly a gift of the gods. Corn on the cob, corn soufflés and puddings, corn tortillas, creamed corn, fried corn—the possibilities seem endless with this versatile vegetable. But Southerners have a special place in their cuisine for two derivatives of corn: cornmeal and grits.

Cornmeal is prepared by grinding corn to the preferred stage of fineness. White cornmeal is usually ground a little finer than yellow, but they can be used interchangeably. Cornmeal, which is a favorite for breading catfish, is also the basis of the South's favorite breads: cornbread and hushpuppies. Cornmeal is available as plain cornmeal; self-rising, which includes baking powder and salt; and self-rising cornmeal mix. Ingredients in the mixes vary and can include baking powder, sugar, and salt. Always read the ingredients on the package and match the ingredients to your recipe.

and Grits

Grits, small flakes of hulled, dried corn, are a staple in the South for breakfast, served with butter or red eye gravy, a thin ham gravy. Never serve grits with sugar and milk! It's definitely not cream of wheat. Grits are also a favorite as a side dish with catfish. Grits sold in most stores are hominy grits, degerminated corn that has been finely ground on steel rollers. Stone-ground grits, whole grain corn ground coarsely on stones, are also available but usually only through mail order or specialty shops.

The secret of cooking grits, whether regular, instant, or quick, is to add the grits slowly to boiling water and to stir frequently while cooking. As you cook and stir, more liquid can be added. For quick cleanup of a sticky grits pan, always use cold water. The grit residue will peel right off the pan.

Anne's Alabama Cornbread

This recipe is made with self-rising cornmeal, and Anne McMahan says that bacon drippings give the bread that down-home Alabama flavor.

Easy
Serves 6 to 8

Cooking spray for pan
4 tablespoons vegetable oil or bacon drippings
1 egg, slightly beaten
2 ½ cups self-rising cornmeal
1½ cups buttermilk

1. Preheat oven to 425° degrees. Spray an 8-inch pan (iron skillet preferred) with cooking spray, coating sides as well.
2. Measure oil or drippings into pan and heat in oven while mixing together egg, cornmeal, and buttermilk.
3. When ingredients are well mixed, pour hot oil into batter and stir well.
4. Pour cornmeal batter into hot pan or skillet and bake until golden brown, approximately 25 minutes.
5. Cut into squares and serve immediately.

Mary Lynn's Never-Fail Cornbread

This recipe from North Carolina is guaranteed to be perfect each and every time. Mary Lynn insists that solid shortening is the only choice for this cornbread.

Moderately Easy
Serves 6 to 8

1 cup all-purpose flour, sifted
¼ cup sugar
4 teaspoons baking powder
½ teaspoon salt
1 cup yellow cornmeal
2 eggs
1 cup milk
¼ cup melted shortening

1. Preheat oven to 425°.
2. Sift flour with sugar, baking powder, and salt. Stir in cornmeal.
3. Add eggs, milk, and melted shortening and beat with an electric or rotary beater until smooth. Be careful not to overbeat. Pour into a greased 9-inch pan (iron skillet preferred.)
4. Bake until golden brown, approximately 20 to 25 minutes. Cut into squares and serve immediately.

Hushpuppies

These hushpuppies will make everyone sit up and beg for more. Hushpuppies are especially good cooked in the hot oil used to fry catfish (or even chicken). For a new and different taste treat, dip hushpuppies in vinegary, Carolina-style barbecue sauce.

Easy
Makes about a dozen

1 cup self-rising cornmeal
½ cup self-rising flour
1 teaspoon sugar
4 tablespoons onion, minced
½ cup milk
1 egg
Oil or shortening for cooking

1. Mix together cornmeal, flour, and sugar.
2. Add minced onion, then blend in milk and egg.
3. Half fill a heavy skillet with oil or shortening and heat to 375°. (A Dutch oven containing at least 1½ inches of oil may also be used.)
4. Drop in a test hushpuppy using two teaspoons, one to scoop the hushpuppy batter and one to push the batter into the hot oil. (Small hushpuppies are better than large ones.) The dough will sink, then rise to the surface when it's done. You may need to thicken or thin your batter with cornmeal or milk so the hushpuppies hold together while cooking.
5. Drop rest of batter slowly into the oil, one teaspoonful at a time, being careful not to spatter hot oil.
6. Drain hushpuppies on paper towels placed on newspaper or a brown paper bag.
7. Put drained hushpuppies on a wire rack placed over a baking sheet and keep hot in a 200° oven while you finish frying the rest of the batter.

Tennessee Hushpuppies

Watch out! These hushpuppies might bite!

Moderately Easy
Serves 6 to 8

2 cups plain cornmeal
1 teaspoon baking powder
1 teaspoon baking soda
¼ teaspoon salt
Black pepper, coarsely ground (to taste)
1 onion, chopped
2 jalapeno peppers, diced
2 cups buttermilk
1 egg
Oil or shortening for cooking

1. Fill a heavy skillet half full of oil or melted shortening and heat to 375° while you make the hushpuppy batter. (A Dutch oven containing at least 1½ inches of oil may also be used, or follow directions on a deep-fat fryer.)

2. Combine cornmeal, baking powder, baking soda, salt, and pepper. Mix well. Add onion and jalapenos.

3. In a separate bowl, whisk buttermilk and egg.

4. Gradually add buttermilk mixture to dry ingredients. Add enough to form a rather stiff batter.

5. When oil reaches the proper temperature, drop in a test hushpuppy using two teaspoons one to scoop the hushpuppy batter and one to push the batter into the hot oil. (Small hushpuppies are better than large ones.) The dough will sink, then rise to the surface when it's done. You may need to thicken or thin your batter with cornmeal or buttermilk so the hushpuppies hold together while cooking.

6. Drop rest of batter slowly into the oil, one teaspoonful at a time, being careful not to spatter hot oil. Cook until golden brown.

7. Drain hushpuppies on paper towels placed on newspaper or a brown paper bag. Put drained hushpuppies on a wire rack placed over a baking sheet and keep hot in a 200° oven while you finish frying the rest of the batter.

Tennessee Baked Cheese Grits

Ann Wooten says this recipe works well with regular or quick grits.

Easy
Serves 4 to 6

1 cup uncooked grits
Water as directed on package
2 cups Cheddar cheese, grated (divided)
2 eggs, beaten
⅛ teaspoon cayenne pepper
1 teaspoon seasoned salt
Dash of hot sauce
⅛ teaspoon paprika

1. Preheat oven to 375°.
2. Cook grits according to package directions.
3. Add 1½ cups of grated cheese to cooked grits. Mix well.
4. Add eggs, pepper, seasoned salt, and hot sauce to grits. Mix well.
5. Pour into greased 1½-quart casserole and top with remaining ½ cup of cheese. Sprinkle with paprika.
6. Bake for 20 minutes.

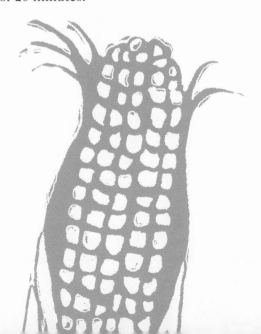

Easy Stovetop Cheese Grits

If you like your grits extra creamy, substitute milk or cream for part of the water. This is also good with a dash of garlic powder or hot sauce added.

Very Easy
Serves 4

Uncooked grits (enough for 4 people)
Water (as directed on package)
1 teaspoon salt
½ teaspoon pepper
2 cups Cheddar cheese, shredded or grated
2 tablespoons butter or margarine
2 to 3 dashes of hot sauce (optional)
1 teaspoon garlic powder (optional)

1. Cook grits according to package directions. Add salt and pepper. (The total amount of salt added is 1 teaspoon, which includes any salt listed in package directions.)
2. When grits are creamy, add cheese and butter. Stir until melted.
3. Add hot sauce and/or garlic powder, if desired.
4. Serve hot. Top with butter, if desired.

11
Sweet Inspirations

A Fitting Climax to Down-Home Cookin' and Uptown Eating

Triple Chocolate Cake   134
Saint Paddy's Day Pie   135
Lemon Icebox Pie   136
Aunt Lila's Pecan Pie   137

Triple Chocolate Cake

This is one of the richest, most sinful cakes to ever grace the dessert table. Sign up for that aerobics class now!

Easy
Many servings!

Cooking spray
Flour (for coating cake pan)
18 ½-ounce chocolate cake mix
2 3 ¾-ounce packages instant chocolate pudding
16 ounces low-fat sour cream
4 eggs
1 cup vegetable oil
12 ounces chocolate chips

1. Preheat oven to 325°. Coat a Bundt pan with cooking spray and dust with flour. Set aside.
2. In a large bowl, combine cake mix, pudding, sour cream, eggs, and oil. Mix lightly until ingredients are combined. The mixture will be very thick. Stir in chocolate chips.
3. Pour into pan. Bake for approximately 1 hour and 15 minutes. Cake is done when a toothpick or cake tester inserted in the center comes out clean or with just a few crumbs attached.
4. Cool on a rack before removing from pan.

Saint Paddy's Day Pie

Ann Barton from Florida serves this on Saint Patrick's Day, but it's sensational any day of the year. This is an extremely rich dessert, and a little goes a long way. If you don't like creme de menthe, try Amaretto, Irish cream, or coffee-based liqueurs or flavorings.

Moderately Easy
Serves 10 to 12

24 Hydrox or Oreo cookies, finely crushed
¼ cup butter or margarine, melted
Cooking spray
¼ cup creme de menthe liqueur or mint flavoring or to taste
7-ounce jar marshmallow cream
16 ounces heavy cream, whipped
Green food coloring

1. Combine crushed cookies and butter or margarine. Press into the bottom of a 9-inch pie pan lightly coated with cooking spray. A springform pan or a pan with a removable bottom works best. Set aside.
2. Gradually add creme de menthe to marshmallow cream, stirring gently.
3. Whip cream until soft peaks form. Slowly fold the whipped cream into the marshmallow/creme de menthe mixture. Add 1 or more drops of green food coloring until you reach the desired shade of green.
4. Pour into crust. Freeze overnight.
5. Before serving, decorate each piece with a dollop of whipped cream, chocolate leaf, and maraschino cherry (optional).

Lemon Icebox Pie

This is a cool and tangy delight on a hot summer day. Note that the filling must be refrigerated for several hours.

> *Easy*
> *Serves 6 to 8*
>
> Vanilla wafers
> 2 egg yolks
> 15-ounce can sweetened, condensed milk
> ½ cup fresh lemon juice
> 1 teaspoon lemon rind, grated
> ½ pint whipping cream
> 2 tablespoons sugar
> ½ teaspoon vanilla

1. Line the bottom and sides of a pie pan with whole vanilla wafers.
2. Beat egg yolks in a nonmetallic bowl. Add condensed milk, lemon juice, and lemon rind. Mix well. Pour into a pie pan. Refrigerate for several hours.
3. When lemon filling is firm, whip cream until soft peaks form. Gradually whip in sugar. Fold in vanilla. Spread whipped cream over pie. Refrigerate until serving time.

HINT: Because raw eggs can convey disease, many cooks choose to bake the pie for approximately 10 minutes at 350°, then refrigerate it.

Aunt Lila's Pecan Pie

Aunt Lila's pecan pie was so well known that it was mentioned during the eulogy at her funeral.

> *Easy*
> *Serves 6 to 8*
>
> 3 eggs
> 1 cup sugar
> ½ bottle Karo pancake syrup (green label)
> ½ cup butter or margarine, melted
> 1 teaspoon vanilla
> 1 cup pecans, chopped
> 1 unbaked pie crust (frozen or homemade)

1. Preheat oven to 350°.
2. In a bowl, combine eggs, sugar, syrup, butter or margarine, and vanilla. Mix well. Add chopped pecans.
3. Pour mixture into unbaked pie crust.
4. Bake for 50 minutes or until a knife inserted into the center of the filling comes out clean.

Notes:

Equivalents and Substitutions

Helpful Hints on What's What

1 pinch equals the amount you can hold between your thumb
and forefinger

1 dash equals 2 to 3 drops

1 tablespoon equals 3 teaspoons

¼ cup equals 4 tablespoons

1 fluid ounce equals 2 tablespoons

4 fluid ounces equal ½ cup or 8 tablespoons

8 fluid ounces equal ½ pint or 1 cup

16 fluid ounces equal 1 pint or 2 cups

32 fluid ounces equal 1 quart or 4 cups

1 stick butter equals ½ cup

2 sticks butter equal 1 cup

1 garlic clove equals ⅛ teaspoon powdered garlic

Juice of 1 lemon equals 2 to 3 tablespoons

1 teaspoon dried herbs equals 1 tablespoon fresh herbs

1 medium jalapeno pepper equals 1 tablespoon chopped jalapeno

1 tablespoon fresh, grated horseradish equals 2 tablespoons prepared
horseradish

1 ounce or square chocolate equals 3 tablespoons cocoa plus
1 tablespoon butter or margarine

1 pound sifted all-purpose flour equals four cups

1 cup bread crumbs equals 4 slices of bread

Index

A

Anne's Alabama Cornbread, 126
Anything-Goes Marinated Salad, 108
Athenian Broiled Catfish, 37
Aunt Lila's Pecan Pie, 137
availability of ingredients, 114

B

baked catfish
    Campfire Catfish, 68
    Catfish Baked in Mushroom-Wine Sauce, 72
    Creole Catfish, 63
    Crispy Catfish, 69
    Herbed Parmesan Catfish, 67
    hints for, 66
    Mexicali Catfish, 40
    Oven Fried Catfish, 20
    Riviera Catfish, 41
    Summer's Garden Catfish, 73
    Sunny Catfish, 70
Basic Barbecue Sauce, 94
Beer-Batter Catfish Fingers, 21
Blackened Catfish, 64
Black-Eyed Pea Salad, 110
Breezy Caribbean Catfish, 33
broiled catfish
    Athenian Broiled Catfish, 37
    Teryaki Catfish, 35
buying and storing catfish, 60

C

Cajun and Creole catfish
    Blackened Catfish, 64
    Catfish Gumbo, 59
    Catfish Jambalaya, 62
    Catfish with Remoulade Sauce, 61
    Creole Catfish, 63
Cake, Triple Chocolate, 134
Campfire Catfish, 68
Carolina Catfish Soup, 78
Catfish Baked in Mushroom-Wine Sauce, 72
Catfish Corn Chowder, 80
Catfish Gumbo, 59
Catfish Isabella, 49
Catfish Jambalaya, 62
Catfish Piccata, 32
Catfish Provençal, 39
Catfish with Remoulade Sauce, 61
cheese
    Easy Stovetop Cheese Grits, 132
    Herbed Parmesan Catfish, 67
    LaDonna's Cheese Strata, 117
    Tennessee Baked Cheese Grits, 131
Cilantro Tartar Sauce, 92
coleslaw
    Moravian, 104
    Oriental, 121
    Quick, 103
cornbread
    Anne's Alabama, 126

Mary Lynn's Never-Fail, 127
cornmeal, facts about, 124
Creole Catfish, 63
Crispy Catfish, 69
curiosities, catfish, 79, 82, 83

D

dips
    Fried Catfish Dip, 100
    Honey-Mustard, 95

E

Easy Italian Grilled Catfish, 52
Easy Poached Catfish, 53
Easy Remoulade Sauce, 90
Easy Stovetop Cheese Grits, 132
equivalents and substitutions, 139
Expandable Catfish Stew, 84

F

farm-raised catfish, 71
fried catfish
    Beer-Batter Catfish Fingers, 21
    Fried Catfish Nuggets, 27
    hints for healthy eating, 28
    New South Fried Catfish, 19
    Oven-Fried Catfish, 20
    Sesame-Fried Catfish, 23
    Spicy Buttermilk-Fried Catfish, 26
    Tempura-Fried Catfish, 24
    Traditional Southern-Fried Catfish, 18
Fried Catfish Dip, 100
Fried Catfish Nuggets, 27
frying catfish, hints for, 16

G

Ginger-Garlic Catfish, 46
Greek Salad, 116
grilled catfish
    Easy Italian Grilled Catfish, 52
    hints for, 44
    Lemon-Basil Grilled Catfish, 51
    Oriental Grilled Catfish, 50
grits
    Easy Stovetop Cheese, 132
    facts about, 125
    Tennessee Baked Cheese, 131
    Herbed Parmesan Catfish, 67

H

herbs and spices
    Cilantro Tartar Sauce, 92
    facts about, 34, 41
    Ginger-Garlic Catfish, 46
    Herbed Parmesan Catfish, 67
    Lemon-Basil Grilled Catfish, 51
    Rosemary Catfish, 47
    storing and using, 88
    Tangy Lime-Peppercorn Catfish, 36
    Yogurt-Dill Sauce, Low-Fat, 98
    Yogurt-Mint Sauce, Low-Fat, 98
Honey-Mustard Dip, 95
Hoppin' John, 111
Horseradish Sauce, Low-Fat, 93
hushpuppies
    Hushpuppies, 128
    Tennessee Hushpuppies, 129

I

Incredibly Easy Breaded Catfish, 48
ingredients, availability of, 114
Italian Tomato Salad, 122

L

LaDonna's Cheese Strata, 117
Lemon Icebox Pie, 136
Lemon-Basil Grilled Catfish, 51
limes
    Tangy Lime-Peppercorn Catfish,
        36
    Tequila-Lime Catfish, 38
literary references to catfish, 54
Low-Fat Horseradish Sauce, 93
Low-Fat Yogurt-Dill Sauce, 98
Low-Fat Yogurt-Mint Sauce, 98
luring catfish, 96
Lynda's Easy Potato Salad, 105

M

Mary Lynn's Never-Fail Cornbread,
    127
Mediterranean Catfish Stew, 81
Mexicali Catfish, 40
microwaved catfish
    Catfish Isabella, 49
    Ginger-Garlic Catfish, 46
    hints for, 44
    Incredibly Easy Breaded Catfish,
        48
    Polynesian Catfish, 45
    Rosemary Catfish, 47
Moravian Coleslaw, 104

N

New South Fried Catfish, 19
oddities, catfish, 79, 82, 83

O

Old-Fashioned Potato Salad, 106
Oriental Coleslaw, 121
Oriental Cucumber Salad, 120
Oriental Grilled Catfish, 50
Oriental Noodle Soup, 83
Oven-Fried Catfish, 20

P

pie
    Aunt Lila's Pecan, 137
    Lemon Icebox, 136
    Saint Paddy's Day, 135
poached catfish
    Easy Poached Catfish, 53
    hints for, 44
pond draining, 102
Polynesian Catfish, 45
potato salad
    Lynda's Easy, 105
    Old-Fashioned, 106
    Tangy, 107

Q

Quick Coleslaw, 103
Quick Tartar Sauce, 91

R

Riviera Catfish, 41
Rosemary Catfish, 47

S

Saint Paddy's Day Pie, 135
salad
    Anything-Goes Marinated, 108
    Black-Eyed Pea, 110
    Greek, 116
    Italian Tomato, 122
    Oriental Cucumber, 120
    South-of-the-Border, 115
    Tuscan Bread, 118
salad, potato *(see* potato salad)
Sandwich, Spicy Catfish, 85
sauce
    Basic Barbecue, 94
    Cilantro Tartar, 92
    Easy Remoulade, 90
    Horseradish, Low-Fat, 93
    mushroom-wine, 72
    Quick Tartar, 91
    Spicy Red, 93
    Summer Salsa, 99
    Tzatsiki, 97
    Yogurt-Dill, Low-Fat, 98
    Yogurt-Mint, Low-Fat, 98
Sesame-Fried Catfish, 23
song references to catfish, 54
soup and stew
    Carolina Catfish Soup, 78
    Catfish Corn Chowder, 80
    Catfish Gumbo, 59
    Catfish Jambalaya, 62
    Expandable Catfish Stew, 84
    hints for making fish stock, 76
    Mediterranean Catfish Stew, 81

Oriental Noodle Soup, 83
South-of-the-Border Salad, 115
spices *(see* herbs and spices)
Spicy Buttermilk-Fried Catfish, 26
Spicy Catfish Sandwich, 85
Spicy Red Sauce, 93
stew *(see* soup and stew)
stock *(see* soup and stew)
storing catfish *(see* buying and
    storing catfish)
substitutions *(see* equivalents and
    substitutions)
Summer Salsa, 99
Summer's Garden Catfish, 73
Sunny Catfish, 70
Sweet Southern Dills, 112

T

Tabouli, 119
Tangy Lime-Peppercorn Catfish, 36
Tangy Potato Salad, 107
Tempura-Fried Catfish, 24
Tennessee Baked Cheese Grits, 131
Tennessee Hushpuppies, 129
Tequila-Lime Catfish, 38
Teriyaki Catfish, 35
Traditional Southern-Fried Catfish,
    18
Triple Chocolate Cake, 134
trivia, catfish, 21, 22, 25
Tuscan Bread Salad, 118
Tzatsiki Sauce, 97

Y

Yogurt-Dill Sauce, Low-Fat, 98
Yogurt-Mint Sauce, Low-Fat, 98